Book 2

Disclaimer

BGS Books and this publication have no association with the Consortium of Selective Schools in Essex (CSSE), or any other schools or examination boards.

Every effort has been made to ensure that the information contained in this book is accurate; however, we are not responsible for anyone failing any part of their exam as a result of the information contained in this book or on our website www.bgsbooks.com

All Rights Reserved

This material has been produced by British Grammar School Books.

Copyright © BGS Books, 2022.

All rights reserved, including translation.

This publication may not be sold or distributed as part of any product or service, including via private tuition. No part of this publication may be stored, reproduced or transmitted in any form or by any means, whether physical or electronic without first obtaining permission from BGS Books. This publication may not be published online, photocopied or otherwise reproduced, including within the terms of any licence granted by the Copyright Licensing Agency Ltd or similar organisations.

Edition 1.0 – Aug 2022

About this Book

Our papers have been written with the intention of providing quality exam question practice at the same standard but slightly higher level of difficulty as the current CSSE 11+ exams.

After each paper is completed, go over the incorrect answers and reattempt at a later date to ensure concept has been understood.

Surname ....

First Name ....

Start Time: ....

End Time: ....

11+ CSSE Stretch

Mathematics Paper 1

40 Minutes

The questions in this paper are worth thirty marks

Attempt all the questions, writing your answers clearly

If you cannot answer a question, leave it, and go on to the next one

Use any time you have left to check your answers and go back to any unanswered questions

The numbers in brackets are the marks available for each question

PAGE	SCORE	
	Marks	Total
2		6
3		4
4		5
5		5
6		6
7		4

Question	ANSWER	MARKS R | T
1 (a) Insert **+**, **-**, **x** or **÷** to make the calculation correct: 15 ☐ 6 = 3 ☐ 7		(1)
(b) Insert a pair of brackets in the expression below to create an answer of 8. 13 − 3 − 2 x 5 = 8		(1)
2 (a) Fill in the missing numbers that complete the calculation: B² - A² = 20 ☐² - ☐² = 20		(1)
(b) Patrick choses a **prime** number. He multiplies it by 10 and then rounds to the nearest hundred. His answer is **300**. List all the prime numbers he could have chosen.		(2)
3 Jack and Jill each start off with the same number. Jack works out half his number and Jill works out three quarters of her number. The sum of their answers is **375**. What number did they both start off with?		(1)

SCORE 6

Question	ANSWER	MARKS R|T

4 This question is about the following five numbers:

$$\frac{7}{10}, \quad \frac{1}{3}, \quad 34\%, \quad 0.352, \quad \frac{6}{15}$$

If they are placed in descending order:

(a) Which number would be fourth in the sequence?

(1)

(b) Which number is closest to 0.349?

(1)

5 Zoe wants to buy 12 bottles of Orange Juice. There are two different offers available:

Fresh World: Buy a pack of 3 bottles for £8.50.

Woolworths: Buy a single bottle for £3.75 and get a bottle free with every 3 you buy.

(a) Which supermarket is cheaper, Fresh World or Woolworths?

(1)

(b) How much more change would Zoe get from a £50 note from the cheaper supermarket compared to the more expensive one?

£

(1)

SCORE 4

Paper 1

Question	ANSWER	MARKS

6 A nautical mile is a measure of distance used for navigation by sea or air.

A distance of 1 nautical mile is equivalent to 1.16 normal miles

A ship sales **5 nautical miles** in in a **time of 43.5 minutes**.

(a) Sailing at the same speed, how many minutes and seconds does it take for the ship to travel 1 nautical mile?

(1)

(b) In minutes and seconds, how long does it take for the ship to sail five normal miles?

(1)

(c) The ship travels another 10 nautical miles in 1 hour and 16.5 mins. What was the ships average speed in **nautical miles per hour**?

nmph (1)

7 The diagram below shows two squares on a straight line.
Calculate the value of **angle 'x'** and **angle 'y'**

X: °

Y: °

(2)

SCORE 5

Paper 1

8 Jadon's fish tank has a length of 80cm, width 50cm and a height which is three quarters of its length.

The tank can hold 1 goldfish for every 10 litres of water.

Jadon buys a 0.36kg pack of fish food for £28.80.

Eat goldfish eats 0.5g of fish food twice a day.

(Tank diagram: 80cm length, 50cm width, Xcm height)

(a) How many litres of water does Jadon need to fill his fish tank?

_____ Litres (1)

(b) The tank can be filled with 200cm³ of water every second. How many minutes will it take to fill the tank?

_____ minutes (1)

(c) Jadon adds the maximum number of fish to the tank. How many does he add in total?

(1)

(d) How many days will a pack last if Jadon feeds all his fish every day.

_____ days (1)

(e) How much does it cost to feed one fish per week?

_____ pence (1)

SCORE 5

Paper 1

9 The rules of a number grid are as follows:

$$A = 2B + C$$
$$D = B + C$$

Where in the diamond: A is top, B is left, C is right, D is bottom.

Using the rules shown, complete the missing numbers in the number grids.

(a) Top = 9, Bottom = 5

(b) Left = 7, Right = 3

(c) Top = 36, Left = 12

(3)

10 Teresa has a shoe size of 4.

Her parents have an average (mean) shoe size of 7.

(a) What is the average shoe size of the family? (1)

(b) The average shoe size of Teresa and her mum is $4\frac{1}{2}$.
Calculate her father's shoe size. (1)

(c) Teresa's shoe size increases by half a size annually.
How many years have passed if the new family average is $7\frac{1}{3}$?

Years (1)

SCORE 6

11 The bar chart compares how much CO_2 six different countries produced in the years 2019 and 2020. All numbers are rounded to the nearest **billion tonnes (BT).**

CO2 Emissions by Country — 2020, 2019

Countries: Germany, Japan, Russia, India, United States, China

(a) Which countries have reduced their CO_2 emissions? (1)

(b) By how many BT did China increase its emissions by? _____ BT (1)

(c) What was the percentage increase in emissions in India? _____ % (1)

(d) If the United States reduces its carbon emissions by the same amount every year, in how many years will it reach zero emissions? _____ Years (1)

SCORE 4

END OF PAPER

Surname ....

First Name ....

Start Time: ....

End Time: ....

11+ CSSE Stretch

Mathematics Paper 2

40 Minutes

The questions in this paper are worth thirty marks

Attempt all the questions, writing your answers clearly

If you cannot answer a question, leave it, and go on to the next one

Use any time you have left to check your answers and go back to any unanswered questions

The numbers in brackets are the marks available for each question

Do NOT use a calculator

PAGE	SCORE	
	Marks	Total
10		5
11		4
12		4
13		4
14		4
15		5
16		4
TOT:		30

Paper 2

Question	ANSWER	MARKS

1 (a) Fill in the box to make the sum work:

$$8\frac{3}{7} \times \boxed{} = 59$$

(1)

(b) Fill in the box to make the sum work:

$$5\frac{2}{4} \div \frac{\boxed{}}{\boxed{}} = 11$$

(1)

2 (a) 5 cm on a map represents 80 miles on the ground. What is the distance between London and Manchester which are 15.5 cm apart on the map?

_____ miles (1)

(b) Basildon and Watford are 32 miles apart. How many cm apart will they be on the map?

_____ cm (1)

3 Two bottles of cola, 1.3 litre each, are shared equally between 25 friends. How much will each person get in millilitres?

_____ ml (1)

SCORE 5

Question 4

Phillip has forgotten the 4-digit pin code on his phone which has numbers 0 to 9.

He remembers the following information:
- The fourth digit is '3'
- The first three digits are even
- The same digit cannot be used more than once

			3

(a) How many code combinations are possible for the three digits?

(1)

(b) The second digit is a cubic number, what is it?

(1)

(c) The third digit is not a factor of the second digit, what is it?

(1)

(d) The sum of the four digits is 19. What is the full four-digit code?

(1)

Paper 2

5 (a) Add together the three lengths of 1.5 km, 1200 m and 510 cm. Provide your answer in kilometres.

Answer: _____ km (1)

(b) Which of the following three volumes is the largest?

1.01 litres, 1,099 ml or 1,101 cm³

(1)

6 Geoffrey plots a pentagon with a line of symmetry through point (11,9).

Points shown on diagram: (11, 9), A, (17, 7), (3, 0), B

(a) What is the coordinate of point A?

(___ , ___) (1)

(b) What is the coordinate of point B?

(___ , ___) (1)

SCORE: 4

Paper 2

7 Emma circles the first eight terms in a number sequence on a grid.

1	2	3	4	5	6	7	8	9	10
11	12	13	14	15	16	17	18	19	20
21	22	23	24	25	26	27	28	29	30
31	32	33	34	35	36	37	38	39	40
41	42	43	44	45	46	47	48	49	50
51	52	53	54	55	56	57	58	59	60
61	62	63	64	65	66	67	68	69	70

(Circled: 1, 2, 3, 5, 8, 13, 34)

(a) Emma has forgotten to circle the 7th term. Which number is this? (1)

(b) What is the 9th term in the sequence? (1)

(c) What is the highest number on the grid that Emma can circle if she continues the sequence? (1)

(d) What is the difference between the 8th term and the sum of all the prime numbers **circled** on the grid? (1)

Paper 2

8 An online shop offers four different appliances for sale.

Appliance	Price	Delivery Charge
Washing Machine	£490	£40
Dishwasher	£370	£45
Fridge	£1100	£90
Tumble Dryer	£400	£35

The delivery charges shown are for weekdays only are per appliance.

The delivery charge is increased by 10% for a delivery on a weekend.

(a) How much more expensive is the Fridge as a percentage compared to the Tumble Dryer?

_____ % (1)

(b) Henry buys a washing machine and dishwasher.
What is the total amount he pays if both items are delivered on Saturday?

£ _____ (1)

(c) Discount vouchers apply only to the items and not the delivery charge. If Henry has a 13% voucher, how much will he save?

£ _____ (1)

(d) Sarah has a 30% discount voucher. Which appliance did she buy if she paid £315 in total including delivery on a Monday?

_____ (1)

SCORE 4

Question	ANSWER	MARKS

9 Susan cycles for 2.25 hours. During that time, Susan takes three breaks, with each break twice as long as the previous one. Her first break was after 30 minutes cycling.

(a) If Susan's total break time was 35 minutes, how long was her shortest break?

min (1)

(b) If Susan started cycling at 16:57, at what time did she end her first break?

(1)

10 Cube A and cuboid B below have **equal** volumes.

A: 6m cube
B: 12m × 6m × x

(a) What is the width 'x' of cuboid B?

m (1)

(b) What is the surface area of cuboid B?

m² (1)

(c) A five-litre tin of paint can cover 20m². Exactly how many litres of paint do I need to cover all sides of cuboid B?

litres (1)

SCORE 5

11 The table below shows the tax band in four towns. The band varies depending on the value of the house. *For example, a house valued at £750,000 in Chelmsford would be classified as a 'Band B' house as it is greater than £750,000.*

House Value	Chelmsford	Colchester	Southend	Westcliff
>= £250,000	Band A	Band A	Band A	Band A
>= £500,000	Band A	Band A	Band B	Band A
>= £750,000	Band B	Band B	Band C	Band C
>= £1,000,000	Band B	Band C	Band D	Band D

The second table shows the monthly tax bill for each band. *For example, in 'Band A', a couple would pay £80 per month, or a student would pay £60 per month.*

Council Band	Single	Student	Pensioner	Couple
Band A	£50	£60	£70	£80
Band B	£70	£80	£89	£93
Band C	£100	£90	£100	£128
Band D	£101	£110	£129	£150

(a) How much tax will a pensioner pay each month for a house worth £740,000 in Colchester?

£ _____ (1)

(b) If a couple pay £80 tax for a house in Southend. What is the lowest amount that their house is worth?

£ _____ (1)

(c) A single person pays £101 monthly tax. How much more would a couple pay living in the same house over 1 year?

£ _____ (1)

(d) Only couples and singles live on Ashton Road. All live in Band A. The couples pay £4,240 a month and the singles £850 a month in tax. How many houses are there on Ashton Road?

(1)

SCORE 4

Surname ....

First Name ....

Start Time: ....

End Time: ....

11+ CSSE Stretch

Mathematics Paper 3

40 Minutes

The questions in this paper are worth thirty marks

Attempt all the questions, writing your answers clearly

If you cannot answer a question, leave it, and go on to the next one

Use any time you have left to check your answers and go back to any unanswered questions

The numbers in brackets are the marks available for each question

Do NOT use a calculator

PAGE	SCORE	
	Marks	Total
18		6
19		5
20		5
21		5
22		4
23		5
TOT:		30

Paper 3

Question	ANSWER	MARKS

1 (a) Calculate the average of

58.7 m and 330 cm

Answer: ___ m (1)

(b) Express as a whole number the median of

5^2, 3^3, 2^5

(1)

(c) Identify the modal value

4^2, 4^3, 2^4, 3^4

(1)

(d) Which two prime numbers when multiplied together equals 91

(1)

2 Ben is using a 'multiply and 'subtract' number machine.

When he inputs 11, the output is 15. When the input is 25, the output is 71.

11 → [x?] → [-?] → 15

25 → [x?] → [-?] → 71

(a) Complete the missing values in the number machine used by Ben.

INPUT → [x ......] → [- ......] → OUTPUT

(1)

(b) Calculate the INPUT if the OUTPUT is 20?

(1)

SCORE: 6

Question	ANSWER	MARKS

3 The line graph shows the cost of delivering parcels in Ireland. Answer the questions.

(a) Complete the following statemen:

The cost of sending parcels up to _____ kg is £ _____

(1)

(b) What is the average cost of delivery for each kg over 10 kg?

£ (1)

(c) What is the cost of posting a 34kg parcel?

£ (1)

4 (a) Harry buys a box of 30 apples for £18. At what price must he sell each apple so that he makes a total profit of £9?

£ (1)

(b) Harry finds five bad apples that he can't sell.
By how much does he need to increase the sale price of each apple to make the same total profit of £9?

£ (1)

SCORE 5

Paper 3

Question	ANSWER	MARKS

5 (a) In an arithmetic test, 4 marks were awarded for each correct answer. Tim achieved a score of 80% with a total mark of 96. How many questions did Tim get wrong?

(1)

(b) Nine cakes were each cut into 8 slices each and put-on sale for £1.20 per slice. If 17 slices were unsold, what was the total value of sales?

£ (1)

6 The jug shown has three different scales and when full can hold 20 oz.

Vera tries to pour 1 cup of milk into the jug.

(a) How many extra ounces did Vera pour into the jug?

Oz (1)

(b) How many more cups does Vera need to fill the jug?

(1)

(c) $1\frac{2}{3}$ cups of milk are needed to make 1 batch of cheese.

How many whole batches of cheese can be made with 3 full jugs?

(1)

SCORE 5

Question	ANSWER	MARKS R T
7 (a) Geraint starts from 3 and counts up in fours. David starts from 60 and counts down in sevens. What is the first identical number that both boys will reach?		(1)
(b) 1 cm on a map represents a distance of 2 km on the ground. What distance in metres is represented by 3 mm on the map?	m	(1)

8 The shape shown is made from two squares.

The smaller shaded square has been rotated at an angle.

Answer the questions below.

4cm

12cm

(a) What is the perimeter of the large square?	cm	(1)
(b) Calculate the total area of the four white sections.	cm²	(1)
(c) How many of the white triangles can fit inside the shaded square.		(1)

SCORE 5

Paper 3

Question | ANSWER | MARKS

9 Joe flies his helicopter along the dotted route below and stops at four locations marked A, B, C and D.

The distance from **A to B** is 22km, **A to C** is 52km and **A to D** is 107km.

(a) If Joe flies at an average speed of 44 km/h from A to B, how long will it take him? Answer in minutes.

mins (1)

(b) If it takes Joe 12 minutes to travel from B to C, what is his average speed? Answer in kilometres per hour.

Km/h (1)

(c) If Joe travels half the speed from C to D as he did from A to B, how many minutes will it take him to get from C to D?

min (1)

(d) What was Joes total average speed from A to D? Ans to 2.d.p.

Km/h (1)

SCORE 4

Paper 3

Question	ANSWER	MARKS R | T

10 A triathlon is a three-sport race consisting of running, cycling and swimming.

Points are awarded for each race and vary depending on time taken.

Example, completing the cycle race in < (less than) 60 mins, wins 40 points.

Cycling (mins)	Running (mins)	Swimming (mins)	Points Awarded
< 60	< 140	< 10	40
60 – 120	140 – 160	< 11	35
121 – 180	161 – 200	< 12	30
> 180	> 200	> 13	10

(a) Jesse completes her cycling in 2 hours 10 mins, running in 2 hours and swimming in 14 mins – what was her total score?

Points (1)

(b) Ed completes his cycling in 60 mins, running in 2 hr 20 mins and swimming in 11 mins – what was his total score?

Points (1)

(c) Ali achieves 100 pts by cycling in 3 hours and running in 2hr 52 mins. In which of the three sports did he score the most points?

(1)

(d) What is Fred's lowest possible points total for cycling if he scored an average of 30 points across all three sports?

Points (1)

(e) Jo scores 3 times as many points in running than swimming.
She scores the same number of points in cycling as in running.
What was her total point score?

Points (1)

SCORE 5

END OF PAPER

Surname ....

First Name ....

Start Time: ....

End Time: ....

11+ CSSE Stretch

Mathematics Paper 4

40 Minutes

The questions in this paper are worth thirty marks

Attempt all the questions, writing your answers clearly

If you cannot answer a question, leave it, and go on to the next one

Use any time you have left to check your answers and go back to any unanswered questions

The numbers in brackets are the marks available for each question

Do NOT use a calculator

PAGE	SCORE	
	Marks	Total
26		5
27		6
28		5
29		4
30		5
31		5
TOT:		30

Paper 4

Question	ANSWER	MARKS R / T
1 (a) Calculate 143.22 - 7.87		(1)
(b) Calculate the difference between the largest and smallest from the list: 1.071, 1.0179, 1.01, 1.0107		(1)
(c) Work out the value of x if $\frac{1}{8} + \frac{1}{24} = \frac{1}{X}$		(1)
2 (a) A school raffle prize of £231 is shared equally between 21 winning tickets. If Elsa had three tickets, how much did she win?	£	(1)
(b) 67.5% of a class of 40 students take a test. It takes 12 minutes to mark one test. How long will it take to mark all the tests? Provide your answer in **hours and minutes**.		(1)

SCORE 5

Paper 4

Question	ANSWER	MARKS

3 Complete the missing numbers in the number chains below.

(a)

7 → 21 → 63 → ……… → 567

(1)

(b)

……… → 50 → 26 → 14 → 8

(1)

(c)

348 → 92 → 28 → 12 → ………

(1)

4 Urwa has a bag of strawberry and bubble-gum flavoured sweets.
She eats half and gives a fifth of what was left to her sister.
Of the remaining 20, she gave three times as much to her mum than her dad

(a) How many sweets did Urwa give to her dad?

(1)

(b) How many sweets did she give to her sister?

(1)

(c) How many sweets did Urwa have to start with?

(1)

SCORE 6

Paper 4

Question	ANSWER	MARKS
5 The clock face below has been drawn with its centre at the coordinates (2, 2) The number '9' on the circumference of the clock has a coordinate of (-4, 2)		
(a) Calculate the coordinates of the number '3' on the clock?		(1)
(b) Calculate the coordinates of the number '6' on the clock.		(1)
(c) The circumference of a circle is calculated as 2 x 3.14 x radius. Calculate the circumference of the clock.		(1)
(d) What is the distance along the circumference between the numbers '12' and '3'?		(1)
(e) A second clock has a radius 50% larger than this clock. What is the diameter of the second clock?		(1)

SCORE 5

6 Four students take part in a sponsored walk for charity.

The total money raised will be shared between two charities called Alpha and Beta in the ratio of 3:1.

Student Name	Miles	Total Money Raised
Oliver	8	£25.60
Anne	7	£26.60
Brett	6	£21.00
Yang	7	£23.80

(a) How much money has been raised for the Alpha Charity?

£ _____ (1)

(b) Which student raised the most money per mile?

_____ (1)

(c) Alpha charity decides to share the proceeds of the charity equally. How much more will Beta charity now get?

£ _____ (1)

(d) A fifth student, Fran, wants to walk 5 miles. How much money will she need to raise to earn as much money per mile as Yang?

£ _____ (1)

Question	ANSWER	MARKS R T

7 Grant wants to lay wooden flooring in his lounge. He draws a floor plan of his apartment using a **scale of 1:50**. Each plank measures 1m length and 20cm wide.

[Floor plan showing: Lounge (3.8m tall, with 2.3m internal measurement), Kitchen (top right area, with width W), Bedroom, Porch (1.0m wide), Hall (1.1m tall). Total top width 6.4m, 5.1m measurement shown.]

(a) The area of the kitchen is 5.98m². Calculate the width 'W' in cm.

cm (1)

(b) Calculate the total area of Grants apartment.

m² (1)

(c) Using the scale, calculate the perimeter of the bedroom in cm.

cm (1)

(d) How many whole planks does Grant need to cover his lounge?

(1)

(e) Planks are sold in packs of five. Each pack costs £12.99. How much will Grant spend to buy the correct number of packs?

£ (1)

SCORE 5

8 Dr Moore wants to take out car insurance. He has two options:

Option 1: Fixed price of £750 per annum with unlimited mileage

Option 2: Fixed price of £280 per annum and then 10p for every 5 miles driven.

(a) Express option 2 as a formula, where the T = Annual Cost in £ and M = mileage driven.

T = ... (1)

(b) If Dr Moore travels 3000 miles using option 2, what is his cost?

£ .... (1)

(c) If Dr Moore paid £880 for the year using option 2, how many miles had he driven?

(1)

(d) How many miles would Dr Moore need to drive so the that options 1 and 2 costs are the same?

(1)

(e) If Dr Moore removes the mileage tracking device from his car, he has to pay a £19 fine per day. Re-write the formula from (a) to reflect this additional charge. The number of days = d.

T = ... (1)

SCORE 5

END OF PAPER

Surname ....

First Name ....

Start Time: ....

End Time: ....

11+ CSSE Stretch

Mathematics Paper 5

40 Minutes

The questions in this paper are worth thirty marks

Attempt all the questions, writing your answers clearly

If you cannot answer a question, leave it, and go on to the next one

Use any time you have left to check your answers and go back to any unanswered questions

The numbers in brackets are the marks available for each question

Do NOT use a calculator

PAGE	SCORE	
	Marks	Total
34		6
35		5
36		7
37		4
38		4
39		4
TOT:		30

Paper 5

Question	ANSWER	MARKS

1 (a) Complete the following fraction:

$$\frac{11}{18} + \underline{} = \frac{8}{9}$$

(1)

(b) Calculate the following and provide the answer in simplest form:

$$-2\frac{1}{4} \times -2\frac{1}{10} =$$

(1)

(c) Calculate the following and provide the answer in simplest form:

$$5\frac{1}{3} \div 5\frac{7}{9} =$$

(1)

2 (a) Calculate 5^3 divided by 3^2. Answer to two decimal places.

(1)

(b) A rabbit grows by 1/8th of its length every month. If it starts off 16cm, how long is it after 2 months?

(1)

(c) Jack ran a mile in 16 minutes. Jill ran 3 minutes faster and started 5 minutes after him. How many minutes after Jack finished the race did Jill finish?

(1)

SCORE: 6

Question	ANSWER	MARKS R | T
3 (a) Convert $\frac{1}{3}$ of nine kilometres squared into metres squared. How many **zeros** is there in the answer?		(1)
(b) Convert 18 km per hour into metres per second	m/s	(1)
4 Andy is driving along the M25. He sees a road sign that says there is another 14 miles to get to Heathrow airport. The maximum speed limit is 70 miles per hour.		
(a) If Andy drives at the maximum speed limit, how long will it take to arrive at the airport?	mins	(1)
(b) Andy reduced his speed by 20% for half the journey. How much longer will it take him to reach the airport?	mins	(1)
(c) In the end, it took them 42 minutes to reach the airport. What was their average speed?	mph	(1)

SCORE 5

Paper 5

Question — ANSWER — MARKS R | T

5 The table below shows what dosage of medicine to administer to children of different age groups from birth to 12. Using this information, answer the questions below.

Age	Timings	Dose
3 to 6 months	Up to 3 times in 24 hours	2.5ml
6 to 12 months	3 times a day	2.5ml
1 to 2 years	3-4 times a day	2.5ml
3 to 7 years	3-4 times a day	5ml
8 to 12 years	3-4 times a day	10ml

Do not give more than 4 doses in any 24 hour period
Leave at least 4 hours between doses.

(a) What is the maximum dose of medicine an 18-month-old child can have in one day?

_____ ml (1)

(b) If one tablespoon holds 5ml of medicine, how many spoons will a 10-year-old have after 3 doses?

(1)

(c) If a 7-year-old had her first dose at 9am, what is the earliest time she can have her 4th and final dose?

(1)

6 There are 20 square and triangle shapes in a bag.

Each is either black or white.

The ratio of black shapes to white shapes is 3:2
The ratio of black triangles to black squares is 1:2
The ratio of black squares to white squares is 4:1

Next to each shape, write down the quantity of each in the bag.

(4)

SCORE 7

7 The chart below shows four different classifications of typing speed.

The more words you can type per minute, the higher the classification of your speed.

(a) Annie writes 600 words in 20 minutes. What classification is she? (1)

(b) What is the minimum number of words Annie needs to achieve a 'Fast' classification within a 20-minute period? (1)

(c) Annie achieves a classification of Advanced. What is the slowest time she could have typed 800 words to achieve this? _____ mins (1)

(d) Adam has two '15 minute' attempts at typing. First, he types 553 words and then 652 words. What classification is he? (1)

8 The two pictures shown below are the third and fourth shape in a sequence made from black and white triangles.

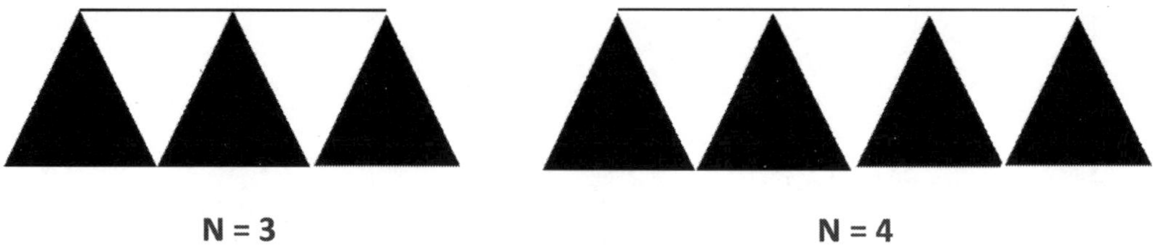

N = 3   N = 4

(a) Write down an expression, in terms of n, for the total number of triangles in the nth shape.

(1)

(b) How many triangles in total would be needed for the 11th shape in the sequence?

(1)

(c) How many black triangles would be needed in the 100th shape?

(1)

(d) The area of each triangle is 15cm².
What is the total area of all the white triangles in the 40th shape?

(1)

Question	ANSWER	MARKS
9 The body mass index (BMI) is calculated by dividing weight by height squared. $$BMI = \frac{Weight}{Height^2}$$ Weight must be in kilograms and Height in Metres.		
(a) Mark is 160 cm tall and has a weight of 64 kg. What is his BMI?		(1)
(b) Rosa has a BMI of 50. Her weight is 32 kg. What is her height in centimetres?	cm	(1)
(c) Giovanni has a BMI of 30. He is 1.7m tall. What is his weight in Kilograms?	Kg	(1)
(d) Stella has a BMI of 32. She is 1.5m tall and weighs 72kg. How much weight must she lose to have achieve a BMI of 30?	Kg	(1)

Paper 5

END OF PAPER

Surname ....

First Name ....

Start Time: ....

End Time: ....

11+ CSSE Stretch

Mathematics Paper 6

40 Minutes

The questions in this paper are worth thirty marks

Attempt all the questions, writing your answers clearly

If you cannot answer a question, leave it, and go on to the next one

Use any time you have left to check your answers and go back to any unanswered questions

The numbers in brackets are the marks available for each question

Do NOT use a calculator

PAGE	SCORE	
	Marks	Total
42	6	
43	5	
44	5	
45	4	
46	5	
47	5	
TOT:	30	

Paper 6

Question	ANSWER	MARKS

1 (a) Two numbers **multiply** together to make −36
They **add** together to make 9

What are these two numbers? (1)

(b) Two equal numbers **subtracted** from each other make 0
They **add** together to make 30

What are these two numbers? (1)

(c) Two fractions **multiply** together to make an eighth
The **add** together to make three quarters

What are these two fractions? (1)

2 In each of the following calculations there is an error, which can be corrected by changing **one digit to the number 3**. In each case identify the digit to be changed.

(a) 6.54 − 2.41 = 1.13 (1)

(b) 27 + 51 + 16 + 8 = 97 (1)

(c) 416 + (3 × 25) = 391 (1)

SCORE 6

Question	ANSWER	MARKS

3 A number machine works by doubling its input, then adding a fifth of the new value before halving the number to give the output.

Example: Input 10: → 20 → 24 → 12 → Output is 12

(a) Calculate the output if the number input is -5

(1)

(b) Calculate the input, if the output number is 18

(1)

4 A toy shop has two special offers for its customers.

10% Discount if spending £50 or more
15% Discount if spending £100 or more

(a) If Ali wants to buy two toys, one for £24.79 and another for £26.81, how much will his bill be after the discount is applied?

£ (1)

(b) If Li Wong's bill is £102 after a 15% discount, what was his bill before the discount?

£ (1)

(c) Elena wants to buy two skateboards for £69.50 each. How much cheaper will it be to buy together instead of separately?

£ (1)

SCORE 5

Paper 6

Question	ANSWER	MARKS

5 The diagram below shows a right-angled triangle and three parallel lines.
Calculate the size of angles A, B and C.

(A) .... °

(B) .... °

(C) .... °

(3)

6 Look closely at the scale below and answer the questions.

(a) Subtract B from C, then, multiply the answer by D.

(1)

(b) The average of D, E & F is not equal to the average of D and F.
Is this statement TRUE or FALSE?

(1)

SCORE 5

Paper 6

Question 7

10:34 NEW YORK   15:34 LONDON   23:34 TOKYO

The clocks show the current local time in New York, London and Tokyo

In each city, the shopping malls open at 7am and close at 8pm local time every day.

(a) When the mall opens in New York, what time is it in Tokyo? (1)

(b) It is 8pm on Thursday in London.
In how many hours will the shopping mall open in Tokyo?

_____ hours (1)

(c) It takes 7 hours and 23 mins to fly from London to New York.
My flight leaves Tuesday at 9:06pm.
What time is it in New York if I landed 15 minutes late? (1)

(d) I arrive back in London on Friday at 9am local time.
How many hours and minutes did I spend in New York?

_____ hours
_____ mins (1)

SCORE 4

Paper 6

Question

Cassy has a cereal box to use as part of a school project.

The dimensions of the box are as follows:

- Length 30cm
- Width is **w** cm
- Depth is **d** cm

Answer all questions below.

8 (a) Write down the expression for volume of the box.

Answer: cm³ (1)

(b) Now write down an expression that sums all the edges of the cereal box. Simplify where possible.

(1)

(c) If the volume of the box is 3750 cm³ and the depth is 5cm. Calculate the width, w.

Answer: cm (1)

(d) Calculate the surface area of the outside of the box.

Answer: cm² (1)

(e) If Casey cuts out the front of the box, leaving only the back and sides, what is the new surface area in m²?

Answer: m² (1)

SCORE: 5

Paper 6

Question

9 Peter buys a pair of trainers from London for £130 and Milan for 153 Euros.

The exchange rate is: **1 British pound (£) = 1.13 Euros (€)**

(a) What is the average price Peter paid for both pairs of trainers? Provide your answer in Euros.

_____ Euros (1)

(b) If I convert €339 to pounds, how much change would I get if I bought two pairs of trainers from London?

£ _____ (1)

10 Two sequences are written out as follows:

Rule	1st term	2nd term	3rd term
Sequence X: add 6 to each term	10	16	22
Sequence Y: subtract 3 from each term	82	79	76

(a) What is the difference between the 5th term of sequence X and the 6th term of sequence Y?

(1)

(b) At what term will sequence X equal sequence Y?

(1)

(c) What is the sum of the 100th term of sequence X & sequence Y?

(1)

SCORE 5

END OF PAPER

Surname ....

First Name ....

Start Time: ....

End Time: ....

11+ CSSE Stretch

Mathematics Paper 7

40 Minutes

The questions in this paper are worth thirty marks

Attempt all the questions, writing your answers clearly

If you cannot answer a question, leave it, and go on to the next one

Use any time you have left to check your answers and go back to any unanswered questions

The numbers in brackets are the marks available for each question

Do NOT use a calculator

PAGE	SCORE	
	Marks	Total
50		5
51		5
52		4
53		6
54		6
55		4
TOT:		30

Paper 7

Question	ANSWER	MARKS

1 (a) Solve 17 - 11 x (9 - 15)

(1)

(b) Solve $6^2 ÷ 2(1 + 2)$

(1)

2 In this question, each blank square can be completed using any single digit from 1 to 9. **Each digit can only be used once in the <u>entire calculation</u>**.
Fill in the squares to complete the calculation.

(a) 1☐ x 8 = 96

(1)

(b) ☐ ÷ ☐ = 4

(1)

(c) 4 x (☐ + ☐) = 28

(1)

SCORE 5

Question	ANSWER	MARKS

3 The fastest land animal in the world is the Cheetah.
It can travel two kilometres in one minute.

(a) What is the speed of the Cheetah in km per hour?

_____ km/h (1)

(b) What is the speed of the Cheetah in metres per second?

_____ m/s (1)

(c) An antelope can travel at 98kph. How much further can a Cheetah travel than an antelope in 2.5 hours?

_____ km (1)

4 (a) The height of a ten-year-old boy is 134.5cm. He grows by 4% after year 1. He then grows a further 3.2cm after another year. What is his new height?

_____ cm (1)

(b) Rebecca is 1.47m tall.
If she is 5% taller than her brother, what is his height?

_____ cm (1)

SCORE 5

Paper 7

Question

5 The graph shows the average height of boys and girls in cm between the ages of 12 and 18.

— Average height boy   - - - Average height girl

(a) From what age is the average height of a boy greater than a girl?

(1)

(b) How much greater is the average height of a boy than a girl at the age of 15?

_____ cm   (1)

(c) Peter is 168cm tall. He is 4cm below his average height. How old is he?

(1)

(d) Andy has the average height of a 14-year-old girl.
Andy should be 15 cm taller to be the average male height.
How old will he be in 2 years' time?

(1)

SCORE: 4

Question	ANSWER	MARKS

6 A school plans a trip for 70 children to the zoo. Each child pays £7. Optional lunch is £5 extra.

(a) Hiring a bus for the trip costs £371. What is the minimum number of children needed to cover the cost of the bus?

(1)

(b) If £540 is collected in total from all seventy children, how many children paid for lunch?

(1)

(c) How much profit did the school make from the trip without including the money paid for lunches?

£ (1)

7 A sunflower grows by 23cm in one month. In its second month, it doubles its height. In its third month, it grows by a third of its new height. In its fourth month, it grows by a quarter of its new height.

(a) How tall is the sunflower in its third month?

cm (1)

(b) How tall is the sunflower in its fourth month?

cm (1)

(c) In the fifth month, the sunflower is 0.92m tall. What fraction has it grown by compared to the prior month's height?

(1)

Paper 7

Question	ANSWER	MARKS R	T

8 Pat works in a shop. Each day she marks her diary with the times she has worked. Each cross (x) represents one hour. On Wednesday she worked 3 hours.

Pat is paid £25 for 3 hours work each day. She is paid an extra £8.21 for each additional hour worked. This is known as overtime.

	9am	10am	11am	12pm	1pm	2pm	3pm	4pm
Mon	X	X	X		X	X		
Tues	X	X	X			X		
Weds		X	X	X				
Thurs					X	X	X	X
Fri	X	X	X			X	X	

(a) How much did Pat earn on Monday?

£ _____ (1)

(b) How much did Pat earn in overtime for the entire week?

£ _____ (1)

(c) How many hours must Pat work in a week to earn £210 assuming she does a minimum of 3 hours each day.

(1)

9 Look at the number sequences below. For each one, write down the formula of the nth term.

(a) 6, 10, 14, 18, 22   (1)

(b) 1, 4, 9, 16, 25   (1)

(c) 2, 7, 12, 17, 22   (1)

SCORE 6

Question	ANSWER	MARKS
		R | T

10 Smile is an Essex photography company. They take photos of people and pets.

For an extra cost, they also provide an option to buy a photo frame and key ring.

Type	Cost per Photo	Cost per Frame
Individual	£8.50	10% of Basic Price
Family	£12.50	15% of Basic Price
School	£6.25	35% of Basic Price
Pets	£7.99	25% of Basic Price

Discounts:
- 10% off total bill for 2 photographs
- 15% off total bill for 3 or more photographs
- No discount for school or pet photographs

(a) Barry wants two photos of his cats, each with frames. How much will he pay?

£ _____ (1)

(b) Harry wants an unframed family photo with his wife and two children. He also wants a separate framed photograph with his parents. How much will he pay?

£ _____ (1)

(c) Sally has 3 children. She wants individual photos for each and one family photo with a Frame. How much does she pay?

£ _____ (1)

(d) Sally cancels the individual photos and gets three school photos instead. How much did Sally save after discounts?

£ _____ (1)

END OF PAPER

Surname ....

First Name ....

Start Time: ....

End Time: ....

11+ CSSE Stretch

Mathematics Paper 8

40 Minutes

The questions in this paper are worth thirty marks

Attempt all the questions, writing your answers clearly

If you cannot answer a question, leave it, and go on to the next one

Use any time you have left to check your answers and go back to any unanswered questions

The numbers in brackets are the marks available for each question

Do NOT use a calculator

PAGE	SCORE	
	Marks	Total
58		6
59		5
60		5
61		5
62		4
63		5
TOT:		30

Paper 8

1 (a) Solve the following:

$4 - 8 \div 2 \times (7 - 11)$

(1)

(b) Solve the following:

$(4 - 8) \div 2 \times 7 - 11$

(1)

(c) Place brackets in the correct positions to make the calculation correct:

$4 - 8 \div 2 \times 7 - 11 = -35$

(1)

2 (a) Jennifer has 220 marbles and Peter has 320 marbles. How many marbles should Peter give to Jennifer so that they both have an equal number?

(1)

(b) How many marbles would Peter need to give Jennifer so that Jennifer has 20 more than him?

(1)

(c) The ratio of marbles between Peter and Jennifer is now 2:3. How many more marbles does Jennifer have than Peter?

(1)

SCORE 6

Question	ANSWER	MARKS R | T

Paper 8

3 Derek wants to lay floor tiles in his kitchen. The length of his kitchen is twice the width. The kitchen includes cupboards 0.8m deep along two sides.

0.8m

7.2m

(a) What is the area of Derek's kitchen floor, excluding cupboards?

m² (1)

(b) Derek buys square tiles 25cm wide, how many whole tiles does he need to tile his kitchen floor?

(1)

(c) Tiles cost £34 per pack and contain 16 tiles. Installation is £500. How much will it cost Derek to tile the floor?

£ (1)

(d) If Derek needs a one litre bottle of glue for every 5m² of tiles. How many bottles of glue does he need to tile his kitchen?

(1)

(e) It takes one person 8 days to tile half the kitchen. How many people would it take to completed in two days?

(1)

Paper 8

4 The table below shows the time in six different capitals around the world.
For example, when it's 12:49 in London, it is 20:49 in Beijing.

London	Thu 12:49	Canberra	Thu 23:49
Beijing	Thu 20:49	Abu Dhabi	Thu 16:49
Washington	Thu 07:49	Wellington	Fri 01:49

(a) What is the time difference between London and Abu Dhabi? (1)

(b) Which two cities have the greatest time difference? (1)

(c) The flight from London to Beijing is 11 hours and 30 minutes. If I take off from London at 12:49 on a Thursday, what local time and day will I land in Beijing? (1)

(d) After a 5-hour wait at the airport, I then fly 11 hours and 3 mins from Beijing to Canberra. What time and day will arrive in Canberra? (1)

(e) What will the time and day be in Washington DC? (1)

SCORE 5

Question	ANSWER	MARKS R / T
5 The number of tennis balls in the diagram shown can be calculated by the formula: $$N = \frac{1}{2}r(r+1)$$ where N = number of tennis balls and r = number of rows. In this example, r = 3 and T = 6		
(a) How many tennis balls are there in 8 rows?		(1)
(b) Re-write the formula without the use of brackets.		(1)
(c) How many balls are there in the 31st row?		(1)
6 Brook has drawn a square on a graph. Point A marks the centre of the square. B (11,14) C (11, 4)		
(a) Write down the coordinates of point A	(__ , __)	(1)
(b) Write down the new coordinates if point C is reflected in the Y axis and then rotated around (0,0) by 270° clockwise?		(1)

Paper 8

Question

The diagram shown is a six-panel fence, each panel is 45cm wide and 2.4m tall.
The top of each panel is made up of an equilateral triangle.
The area of the rectangular portion of each panel is 0.9m²

7 (a) What is the height of the rectangular portion of each panel?

_____ m (1)

(b) What is the area of the triangular portion of each panel?

_____ m² (1)

(c) A tub of paint covers 5m². How many tubs are required to paint both sides of the fence?

(1)

(d) One tub of paint costs £10.99. If I have fifteen fence panels around my garden, how much will it cost to paint both sides of the fence with two coats of paint?

£ _____ (1)

SCORE 4

Question	ANSWER	MARKS
8 Anne will turn 45 on the 26th of May 2034.		
(a) How old was Anne on May 25th 2022?		(1)
(b) In what year was Anne born?		(1)
(c) Chris will be half of Anne's age on 26th May 2034. How old would Chris be in years and months on this date?		(1)
(d) Ben is exactly 8 years younger than Chris. In what year did Chris turn 11?		(1)
(e) What is the combined age in years of Anne, Ben and Chris on 26 May 2024?		(1)

Paper 8

END OF PAPER

Surname ....

First Name ....

Start Time: ....

End Time: ....

11+ CSSE Stretch

Mathematics Paper 9

40 Minutes

The questions in this paper are worth thirty marks

Attempt all the questions, writing your answers clearly

If you cannot answer a question, leave it, and go on to the next one

Use any time you have left to check your answers and go back to any unanswered questions

The numbers in brackets are the marks available for each question

PAGE	SCORE	
	Marks	Total
66		5
67		5
68		5
69		7
70		4
71		4

Paper 9

Question	ANSWER	MARKS (R/T)
1 (a) Multiply the answers of 50% of 54 and a quarter of 54.		(1)
(b) Calculate: 21.5 - 6.9 ÷ 3 + (0.32 + 11.68)		(1)
(c) What fraction is half way between $\frac{5}{13}$ and $\frac{6}{13}$? Provide the answer in its simplest form.		(1)
2 How many $\frac{3}{14}$m pieces of wood can be cut from a plank $3\frac{3}{7}$ m long?		(1)
3 Adam is 29 years older than his son. The sum of their ages is 67. How old is Adam?		(1)

SCORE 5

Question	ANSWER	MARKS R | T
4 A whole number X gets rounded to the nearest 100 to give 700. A whole number Y gets rounded to the nearest 10 to give 550.		
(a) What is largest possible value of 2XY?		(1)
(b) What is the smallest possible value of Y ÷ X expressed as a fraction?		(1)
5 The local library is open seven days a week. All books must be returned within 5 days. *For example,* a book borrowed on Monday must be returned by Friday at the latest. The charges for late returns are shown below and capped at £3.50 per item. **Books:** *30p per day after the due date* **CD's:** *40p per day after the due date*		
(a) How much in fines will Peter pay if he returns two books 5 days late and three CD's 8 days late?	£	(1)
(b) Li borrows two books on the 14th of July. She returns one on the 20th July and the other on the 3rd of Aug. How much is her fine?	£	(1)
(c) Clint is charged £3.90 when returning three books and a CD on Mon 4th of April. When did he take these books out on loan?		(1)

Paper 9

Question	ANSWER	MARKS

6 At Royal Grammar school, for every 14 girls, there are 2 more boys.
The ratio of teachers to pupils is 1:15.

(a) Write down the ratio of girls to boys in its simplest form. (1)

(b) If there are 84 girls in Belmont school, how many pupils are there in total? (1)

(c) What is the minimum number of teachers the school can have? (1)

7 Thirty 10p coins are lined up side by side. A third of the coins are replaced by 20p coins and another third replaced with a 50p coins.

(a) What is the total value of coins after all the changes? £ (1)

(b) The remaining 10p coins are now replaced by a new set of coins so that the total value is now £7.20. What is the new coin? (1)

SCORE 5

Question	ANSWER	MARKS

8 Complete the diagram so that the three numbers in each line add up to 12.5.

(4)

9 Study the sequential pattern made from white and grey squares.

The sequence continues.

Complete the blank cells in the table.

Number of White Squares	Number of Grey Squares
10	_____
_____	70
50	_____

(3)

Paper 9

10 The table below shows the price list for different sized flyers.
A discount is applied only to quantities over 50.

e.g., 50 A3 flyers will cost 25p each and any additional ones will cost 15p each

A3 Flyer	1 to 50, 25p each, over 50, 15p each
A4 Flyer	1 to 50, 21p each, over 50, 18p each
A5 Flyer	1 to 50, 15p each, over 50, 12p each
A6 Flyer	15p each
Colour	Additional 60p for every 10 prints on all sizes

(a) Claire wants to order 40 A3 flyers, 60 A4 flyers and 20 A5 flyers. How much will she pay?

(1)

(b) If Claire wants to order colour copies instead, how much extra will she need to pay?

(1)

(c) The company want to charge one price instead of two for all orders of 250 A3 flyers. What price should they charge per flyer so the average cost remains the same?

(1)

(d) All prices shown include 20% tax. How much profit does the company make on 250 A3 Flyers if the cost of each print is 5p?

(1)

SCORE 4

Question	ANSWER	MARKS R	T
11 The weight of a round glass fish bowl depends on its height, radius and thickness. The weight can be calculated using the formula: $$\text{Weight (g)} = \frac{\text{Height (cm)} \times \text{Radius (cm)} \times 0.5}{\text{Thickness (mm)}}$$ The units for each measurement are provided in brackets ()			
(a) What is the weight of a bowl, whose height is twice its radius of 7cm and thickness of glass is 2mm?	g		(1)
(b) What is the radius of a bowl whose weight is 0.3kg, thickness is 3mm and height is 30cm?	cm		(1)
(c) What is the thickness of a bowl that has a weight of 50g, a radius of 200mm and a height of 40cm?	mm		(1)
(d) A bowl contains 800g of oranges and 1.1kg of apples. Both the height and radius is 35cm. The thickness is 1cm. What is the total weight of the bowl including the fruit to 2 decimal places?	KG		(1)

END OF PAPER

Surname ....

First Name ....

Start Time: ....

End Time: ....

11+ CSSE Stretch

Mathematics Paper 10

40 Minutes

The questions in this paper are worth thirty marks

Attempt all the questions, writing your answers clearly

If you cannot answer a question, leave it, and go on to the next one

Use any time you have left to check your answers and go back to any unanswered questions

The numbers in brackets are the marks available for each question

PAGE	SCORE	
	Marks	Total
74		5
75		5
76		5
77		5
78		6
79		4
TOT:		30

Paper 10

1 (a) Workout the following and provide the answer in simplest form:

$$1\tfrac{1}{3} \times 2\tfrac{7}{10} =$$

(1)

(b) Workout the following and provide the answer in simplest form:

$$3\tfrac{2}{3} \div 3\tfrac{6}{15} =$$

(1)

(c) Workout the following and provide the answer in simplest form:

$$7\tfrac{1}{12} - \tfrac{7}{10} =$$

(1)

2 After 7 minutes Fred has walked a quarter of the distance from home to school. After walking another 35 metres, he has walked a third of the distance from home to school in total.

How far is Fred's home from school?

_____ m (1)

3 Abe cuts a piece of string into two pieces. The first piece is 8cm longer than the second piece.

A quarter of the second piece of string is 2cm long.

How long was the total piece of string to start with?

_____ cm (1)

SCORE 5

Question	ANSWER	MARKS

4 The cost of hiring a sailing boat is broken down below:

- Mandatory cost of lifejacket per person = £5
- Cost for first 30 min boat hire = £13.20 (Max 5 per boat)
- Cost for each additional 15 minutes thereafter = £0.80

Note: Additional time can only be bought in blocks of 15 mins

(a) How much will it cost a family of 4 to hire a boat for 2.3 hours?

£   (1)

(b) If it costs three friends £29.80 to sail, for how long did they hire the boat?

Hours

Mins   (1)

(c) Six friends sail for 2 hours exactly.
If they split the total cost equally, how much will each pay?

£   (1)

(d) A party of 15 hire boats. The first boat is hired for 1 hour, the second boat for 85 minutes and the third boat for half an hour longer than the first. How much did they pay altogether?

£   (1)

(e) Wesley wants to hire a boat to travel to an island 39 minutes away. If he wants to spend 45 minutes on the island before returning the boat. How long must he hire the boat for?

Hours

Mins   (1)

Paper 10

Question	ANSWER	MARKS R T

5 The diagram below shows a square with a side length of 8cm. It is surrounded by 8 identical trapeziums. The longest length on the trapezium is also 8cm.

(a) Calculate the total area of the shaded parts of the diagram.

cm² (1)

(b) Calculate the area of one trapezium.

cm² (1)

(c) Calculate the perimeter of the outer square shown in the diagram

cm (1)

6 There are 1.7 pints in a litre and 3.8 litres in a gallon.

(a) How many pints are there in 5 gallons?

(1)

(b) What is the difference in litres between 8.5 pints and 3 gallons?

(1)

SCORE 5

Paper 10

Question	ANSWER	MARKS

7 A website sells a pack of four batteries for £6.00. A pack cannot be split. The table below shows the discounted price when buying multiple packs. For example, buying 7 packs will save you 6% i.e., 36p saving per pack.

Number of Packs	Price per Pack	Saving per Pack
1 to 5	£6.00	0%
6+	£5.64	Save 6%
10+	(a)	Save 8%
15+	£5.46	(b)

(a) How much will eleven packs cost?

£   (1)

(b) Fifteen or more packs cost £5.46.
What is the percentage saving per pack?

(1)

(c) How much will I spend in total if I need 45 batteries?

£   (1)

8 (a) Round each number below to the nearest hundredth and place the new number in decreasing order.

2.317,   2.249,   2.599,   2.286,   2.573

_____ , _____ , _____ , _____ , _____

(1)

(b) A 3-decimal number is rounded to 15.5.
What is the smallest number this could have been?
Answer to 3 decimal places.

(1)

Paper 10

9 The table shows the time it took for four men and women to complete a marathon in hours and minutes.

| Men | 2hr 21m | 2hr 37m | 2hr 31m | 2hr 19m |
| Women | 2hr 24m | 2hr 22m | 2hr 31m | 2hr 27m |

(a) What was the average men's time in hours and minutes? (1)

(b) What was the average time of the fastest two runners? (1)

(c) A fifth female is included in the race. Her time reduces the overall average by 4 minutes. What position will she be? (1)

10 Gemma writes the numbers 1 to 25 on a piece of paper.
Using these numbers only, answer the following:

(a) Subtract the largest prime number from the largest square number. (1)

(b) Multiply the largest cube number by the third largest square number. (1)

(c) How many pairs of prime numbers sum up to a square number? (1)

11 Cara records the number of cars that pass by her house every minute.

(a) What was the least number of cars to pass by in any one minute?

(1)

(b) What was the highest number of cars to pass by per minute?

(1)

(c) How many cars passed by in total?

(1)

(d) How many minutes in total did Cara record the number of cars passing by her house?

(1)

END OF PAPER

Surname ....

First Name ....

Start Time: ....

End Time: ....

11+ CSSE Stretch

Mathematics Paper 11

40 Minutes

The questions in this paper are worth thirty marks

Attempt all the questions, writing your answers clearly

If you cannot answer a question, leave it, and go on to the next one

Use any time you have left to check your answers and go back to any unanswered questions

The numbers in brackets are the marks available for each question

PAGE	SCORE Marks	Total
82		5
83		5
84		6
85		4
86		6
87		4
TOT:		30

Paper 11

Question	ANSWER	MARKS R / T
1 (a) A whole number is doubled then rounded to the nearest 100 to give 1500. What is the smallest possible value X could be?		(1)
(b) A and B are whole numbers. B is twice the size of A. When A and B are added together the result is 24. What is the value of A?		(1)
(c) C and D are whole numbers. When C is subtracted from D, the result is 20. When C is added to D, the result is 40. What is the value of C x D?		(1)
2 This question is about three positive whole numbers, E, F and G. We know that **E + F = G** and **E ÷ G = 3**		
(a) What is the value of G if (E + F) + (G - E) = -7?		(1)
(b) What is the value of F?		(1)

SCORE 5

Question	ANSWER	MARKS

3 Billy has a 12-hour clock on his bedroom wall.

The hour hand is on 7 and the minute hand is on 21.

(a) What is the size of the smallest angle between the hour hand and minute hand?

(1)

(b) If the minute hand turns by 840°, what is the new time?

(1)

(c) Through what angle will the hour hand have turned between 9pm and 1am?

(1)

(d) Between the times of 9:36pm and 2:34am, how many times will the minute hand have passed by the number 07?

(1)

4 Ted spent two thirds of his savings on a new phone.

He then spent half of what was left over on new shoes.

If Ted has £55 remaining, how much did he have to begin with?

£   (1)

Paper 11

Question	ANSWER	MARKS R / T
5 Harry, George, Fred and Mike ordered 3 pizzas. Each Pizza has 6 slices. Harry ate half a pizza. George ate a third. Fred ate a third less than Mike. Mike ate twice as much as Harry.		
(a) How much more pizza did Mike eat than George? Express your answer as a fraction.		(1)
(b) How many slices did the boys eat in total?		(1)
(c) Who ate the least pizza?		(1)

6

Using the information Y = 2X, B=X and 2C = Z, calculate the size of the angles marked A, B and C.

A:

B:

C:

(3)

SCORE 6

Question	ANSWER	MARKS

7 300 Children were given the choice to eat either an orange or an apple.

For each of the statements below, state if they are **True** or **False**.

100 Boys   ■ Oranges   200 Girls
■ Apples

(a) Three quarters of the girls ate apples. (1)

(b) The boys ate the same number of apples as the girls ate oranges. (1)

(c) Three times as many boys ate apples as compared to girls. (1)

(d) Altogether, 175 children ate oranges. (1)

Paper 11

8. The table below shows the exchange rate for one Euro (€).
Use this information to answer the questions below.

Currency	Exchange Rate
US Dollars ($)	1.25
Swiss Francs (CHF)	1.00
GB Pounds (£)	0.88

(a) Two friends buy a meal deal for $7.99 each. How many Euros will this cost? (1)

(b) The friends have $220 left to spend in Switzerland. How many Swiss Francs will they get? (1)

(c) At the end of their trip, the friends have 23 CHF, €42 and $19.43 left over. How much do they have in USD? (1)

9. Fran has a reel of ribbon two metres long and 5 cm wide.

(a) Fran cuts half the ribbon into 16 pieces, how long is each piece? _____ cm (1)

(b) He then cuts 50cm of ribbon into 2.5cm each. How many pieces are there? (1)

(c) Fran cuts the remaining piece of ribbon into 3 pieces. If the ratio is 2:3:5, what is the difference between the longest and shortest pieces? _____ cm (1)

SCORE 6

Question	ANSWER	MARKS R T
10 Two shapes with the same diameter are placed 1cm apart each other. Their centres are 7cm apart.		
(a) What is the radius of one circle?	cm	(1)
(b) Find the angle x in the shape above.	°	(1)
(c) What is the distance between the two furthest points, A to B?	cm	(1)
(d) The circumference of a whole circle = 2 x 3.14 x radius (in cm). The distance from B to C = 4.5 cm What is the combined perimeter of both shapes?	cm	(1)

SCORE 4

END OF PAPER

Surname ....

First Name ....

Start Time: ....

End Time: ....

11+ CSSE Stretch

Mathematics Paper 12

40 Minutes

The questions in this paper are worth thirty marks

Attempt all the questions, writing your answers clearly

If you cannot answer a question, leave it, and go on to the next one

Use any time you have left to check your answers and go back to any unanswered questions

The numbers in brackets are the marks available for each question

Do NOT use a calculator

PAGE	SCORE	
	Marks	Total
90		5
91		4
92		4
93		4
94		4
95		5
96		4
TOT:		30

Paper 12

Question	ANSWER	MARKS

1 Esmerelda writes down three different sequences of numbers.

(a) In her first sequence, she adds the same amount each time. Write the missing numbers. (1)

17 , ___ , ___ , ___ , ___ , 52

(b) In her second sequence, each number is the multiple of the previous two numbers. Write the missing numbers. (1)

___ , 5 , ___ , 60 , 900

2 Giles has four hens. All the hens lay eggs on day 1, which begin hatching on day 21.

The Black hen lays 3 eggs every day.
The White hen lays 5 eggs every day.
The Red hen lays 2 eggs every other day.
The Brown hen lays 4 eggs every third day.

(a) How many eggs were laid on the 5th day? (1)

(b) How many eggs will the black hen have hatched by day 28? (1)

(c) On the day six, Giles sells one hen. The next day he collects twelve eggs. Which hen did he sell? (1)

SCORE 5

Question	ANSWER	MARKS R T

3 Evans cycle shops sell 350 bikes in the month of August.

Cereal	Cycles Sold	Cost Price	Sale Price
Muddyfox	49	£110.00	£121.00
Pazazz Cycles	63	£129.00	£193.50
Townsend	98	£104.00	£119.60
Chicco Bikes	35	£140.00	£147.00
Pedal Pals	105	£99.00	£118.80
Total	**350**		

(a) What percentage of the total number of bikes sold were Pedal Pals?

(1)

(b) What is the percentage profit on the sale of each Townsend bike? Answer to 2.d.p.

(1)

(c) Which bike contributed the highest to August sales, Pazazz or Townsend?

(1)

(d) Which two bikes account for 40% of the total bike sold?

(1)

SCORE 4

Paper 12

Question	ANSWER	MARKS R / T

4 The isosceles triangle below has the coordinates A (3,5) and B (7,12).

(a) What are the coordinates of point C? (1)

(b) What are the new coordinates of point A if reflected in the y-Axis? (1)

(c) What are the coordinates of point B if rotated 270° clockwise around the point (0,0)? (1)

(d) What are the coordinates of the middle of the triangle? (1)

SCORE 4

Paper 12

5 Tim has five identical Lego bricks.

They are each 6cm long and have a square edge of 9cm².

He connects his bricks together to build a model as shown in the diagram below.

(a) How long is the model?

_____ cm (1)

(b) What is the volume of the model?

_____ cm³ (1)

(c) What is the surface area of the model?

_____ cm² (1)

(d) Tim puts together more bricks using the same pattern.
The length of the model is now 138cm wide.
How many bricks has Tim used?

(1)

SCORE 4

Question

6 Barry adds screen wash into his car twice a year. He has to mix different amounts with water according to the instructions on the bottle.

His carwash tank has a capacity of 1.5 litres

Season	Water	Screen Wash
Winter	3 parts	1 part
Summer	5 parts	1 part

(a) In winter how many litres of water should Barry add to screen wash to completely fill his water tank?

_____ litres (1)

(b) In summer how much screen wash should Barry add to water to completely fill his water tank?

_____ ml (1)

(c) In summer, Barry's car wash tank is 1/3 full.
How much water should he add to the mixture to fill his tank?

_____ ml (1)

(d) If Barry wants to make his screen wash last longer, should he use the winter mixture or the summer?

(1)

SCORE 4

Question	ANSWER	MARKS
7 (a) How many mm is there in 142.33m?	mm	(1)
(b) A pack of biscuits weighs 80g and two packs of teabags weigh 3/4 the weight of a pack of biscuits. What is the total weight?	g	(1)
(c) A crate of oranges weighs 23kg when full and 9kg when 1/3 full. What is the weight (w) of the crate when empty?	Kg	(1)
8 A cyclist went up 9 miles up a hill at 15 miles per hour. She then cycled down at twice the speed.		
(a) How many minutes did the journey take?	min	(1)
(b) What was her average speed for the full journey?	mph	(1)

SCORE 5

Paper 12

9 The 'Expansion' of a two-digit number is obtained as follows:

The 'Expansion' of 24 is 16 because 2 x 2 x 2 x 2 = 16

and the 'Expansion' of 36 is 729 because 3 x 3 x 3 x 3 x 3 x 3 = 729

(a) Write down the 'Expansion' of the two-digit number 53.

(1)

(b) Which two-digit number was 'Expanded' to give the number 81?

(1)

(c) Identify another two-digit number with the same 'Expansion' of 43.

(1)

(d) A particular two-digit number was 'Expanded'. The answer to this was then also 'expanded'. If the final answer is 9, what was the original number to begin with?

(1)

SCORE 4

ANSWERS

Paper 1

Qn	Part	Answer	Explain
1	a	15 **+** 6 = 3 **x** 7	15 + 6 = 21 and 3 x 7 = 21
1	b	13 – (3 – 2) x 5 = 8	13 - 1 x 5, using BODMAS, 13 - 5 = 8
2	a	$6^2 - 4^2$	36 - 16 = 20
2	b	29 and 31 (2 marks)	29 x 10 = 290, rounded to nearest 100 = 300 31 x 10 = 310, rounded to nearest 100 = 300 23 rounds to 200 and 37 rounds to 400, so not valid answers
3	a	300	$\frac{3}{4}X + \frac{1}{2}X = 375$, so $\frac{5}{4}X = 375$, therefore X= 300
4	a	34%	Descending order: $\frac{7}{10}, \frac{6}{15}, 0.352, 34\%, \frac{1}{3}$ Descending order in decimals: 0.7, 0.4, 0.352, 0.34, 0.333
4	b	0.352	0.34 - 0.349 = -0.009 0.352 - 0.349 = 0.003, therefore closer to 0.0349
5	a	Woolworths	Fresh World = (£8.50 for 3 bottles) x 4 packs = £34 Woolworths (£3.75 for 9 bottles) + 3 free = £33.75
5	b	£0.25	The question asks how much <u>more</u> change, not how much change. Therefore £34 - £33.75
6	a	8 mins 42 seconds	43.5 minutes ÷ 5 nautical miles = 8.7 minutes 0.7 minutes = 0.7 x 60 = 42 seconds
6	b	37 mins 30 seconds	5 nautical miles = 5 x 1.16 normal miles = 5.8 miles 5.8 miles = 43.5mins 1 mile = 43.5 ÷ 5.8 = 7.5 mins **per mile**, x 5 miles = 37.5 mins
6	c	7.5 nautical mph	Total Distance = 5 + 10 = 15 nautical miles Total Time = 43.5 mins + 76.5 mins = 2 hours Speed = Distance/Time = 15 / 2 = 7.5
7	X	65°	Two angles are part of the square, 360° - 90° - 90° - 115°
7	Y	55°	First calculate angle adjacent to Y: 180 - 30 - 115 = 35 Then, 180 - 35 - 90 = 55
8	a	240 litres	Volume = 80 x 50 x $\frac{3}{4}$ of 80 = 240,000 = 240 litres
8	b	20 minutes	240,000 ÷ 200 = 1,200 seconds ÷ 60 = 20 minutes
8	c	24	240 litres ÷ 10 litres per fish = 24 fish
8	d	15 days	Each fish eats 0.5g x2 a day, therefore 24g per day for all fish. 360g ÷ 24 = 15 days
8	e	56 pence	360 grams = £28.80 1 gram = £28.80 ÷ 360 = 8p per gram We know a fish eats 1g per day, so 1 week = 7g of food 7 x 8p = 56p

Paper 1

Qn	Part	Answer	Explain
9	a	4 and 1	C = D - B, substitute this into A = 2B + C. We know A=9, D = 5. 9 = 2B + (D-B), so B = 9 - D, so B = 4 and C = 1
9	b	17 and 10	B = 7, C = 3. So A = 2(7) + 3 = 17 D = 7 + 3 = 10
9	c	12 and 24	C = A - 2B, so 36 - 2(12) = 12 D = B + C = 12 + 12 = 24
10	a	6	Each parent will have a shoe size of 7, so (7 + 7 + 4) ÷ 3
10	b	9	We know the family sum of shoe size is 7 + 7 + 4 = 18* Mum and Teresa = $4\frac{1}{2} + 4\frac{1}{2}$ = 9, therefore 18 - 9 = 9
10	c	8 Years	Sum of new size = 3 x $7\frac{1}{3}$ = 22. This is 4 higher than *18, therefore a difference of 4 sizes. Each year = 0.5, therefore 8 years have passed to grow 4 sizes
11	a	Germany and United States	Only Germany and US 2020 bars are shorter than their 2019 bars
11	b	6.5 BT	2019 = 3.25, 2020 = 9.75. This is a difference of 6.5
11	c	150 %	(2.5 - 1) ÷ 1 x 100 = 150
11	d	7 Years	US had reduced its emissions by 0.75 BT 5.25 ÷ 0.75 = 7 Years

Paper 2

Qn	Part	Answer	Explain
1	a	7	59 ÷ $\frac{59}{7}$ = 59 x $\frac{7}{59}$
1	b	$\frac{1}{2}$	$\frac{22}{4}$ ÷ 11 Note, $5\frac{2}{4}$ is exactly half of 11
2	a	248 miles	1 cm = 16 miles, 15.5 x 16 =
2	b	2 cm	$\frac{5}{80}$ x 32 = 2
3	-	104 ml	2600 ml ÷ 25 = 104
4	a	60	Multiply the number of possible outcomes for the first number by the number of possible outcomes for the second number. Repeat for the third number, 1st number could be 0,2,4,6 or 8 i.e., 5 outcomes 2nd number could be any 4 of the above as 1 no. can't repeat No. of outcomes = 5 x 4 x 3 = 60
4	b	8	8 is the only even cubic number from the choice of 0 to 9
4	c	6	2, 4 and 8 are factors of 8, leaving just the number 6
4	d	2863	19 – 8 – 6 – 3 = 6, so 1st digit is 2

Paper 2

5	a	2.7051 km	1200m = 1.2m and 510cm = 0.0051 1.5 + 1.2 + 0.0051 = 2.7051
	b	1,101 cm³	1.01l x 1000 = 1010ml A cubic cm is equal to a ml, 1,101cm³ = 1101ml > 1099ml
6	a	(5, 7)	17 - 11 = 6, therefore the X axis is a further 6 units back Y = 7 because point A is symmetrical to point (17,7)
	b	(19, 0)	11 - 3 = 8, therefore X = 11+ 8 = 19 Y = 0
7	a	21	The nth term is equal to the sum of the previous to terms Therefore, 7th term = 5th term + 6th terms = 8 + 13 = 21
	b	55	9th term = 7th term + 8th terms = 21 + 34 = 55
	c	55	10th term = 55 + 34 = 89 which is not on the grid, so the 9th term is the highest number available on the grid
	d	11	Sum of prime numbers circled on the grid is 2+3+5+13 = 23 34 - 23 = 11
8	a	175 %	1100 - 400 = 700. 700 ÷ 400 = 1.75 x 100 = 175%
	b	£953.50	Weekday delivery change = 40 + 45 = £85 + 10% = £93.50 £490 + £370 = £860 + £93.50 = £953.50
	c	£111.80	13% discount of £860 (not including delivery) = £111.80
	d	Tumble Dryer	400 x 0.7 = £280 after 30% discount 280 + 35 delivery = £315
9	a	5 minutes	If shortest break = x, then total break time = x +2x + 4x = 7x 35 mins = 7x, so x = 5 minutes
	b	17:32	16:57 + 30 min cycling + 5 min break = 17:32
10	a	3 m	Volume of A = 6 x 6 x 6 = 216 m³ X = 216 ÷ 12 ÷ 6 = 3
	b	252 m²	2 x (36 + 72 + 18) = 252 m²
	c	63 litres	5 litres can cover 20m², therefore 1 litre covers 4m² 252 ÷ 4 = 63 litres
11	a	£70	A £740k house in Colchester falls under band A NOT B A pensioner in Band A pays £70
	b	£499,999	A couple paying £80 will fall under band A Band A in Southend starts at >= 250,000 Band B starts at £500,00, so the max of Band A = £499,999
	c	£588	A single paying £101 will be band D. A pensioner in same band will pay £150, therefore the difference between the two is £49 x 12 months = £588
	d	70 houses	Couples: £4240 ÷ 80 per month = 53 houses Singles: £850 ÷ 50 per month = 17 houses

Paper 3

1	a	31 m	(58.7m + 3.3m) ÷ 2 = 31
	b	27	Median is the middle number 5^2 = 25, 3^3 = 27, 2^5 = 32 = 32
	c	16	4^2 = 16, 4^3 = 64, 2^4 = 16, 3^4 = 81
	d	7 and 13	7 x 13 = 91
2	a	x 4 → − 29	Using logic, 25 needs to multiplied by a no. to get close to 71. Multiple 25 by 4 to get 100, then 71 − 100 = −29. Check: (11 x 4) − 29 = 15
	b	12.25 or $12\frac{1}{4}$	Reverse calculate, so 20 + 29 = 49, then 49 ÷ 4 = 12.25
3	a	10 kg is £5	
	b	£1	For every 5kg increase on the graph, the price increases by £5
	c	£29	30kg = £25, 4 additional kg is £4
4	a	£0.90	Cost of each apple with profit = (£18 + £9) ÷ 30 apples = 90p
	b	£0.18	Cost of each apple with profit = (£18 + £9) ÷ 25 apples = £1.08. Increase in price = 1.08 − 90 = 18p
5	a	6	80% = 96 marks, divide by 4 to determine how many marks equate to 20% = 24 marks. 1 answer = 4 marks, so 24 marks = 6 questions
	b	£66	9 cakes x 8 slices = 72 slices less 17 unsold = 55 slices. 55 x £1.20 = £66
6	a	2 oz	
	b	$1\frac{1}{4}$	$2\frac{1}{2} - 1\frac{1}{4} = 1\frac{1}{4}$
	c	4	3 jugs = 3 x 2.5 cups = 7.5 cups ÷ $1\frac{2}{3}$ = 4.5 batches. Note: 4.5 is incorrect as question asks for whole batches
7	a	11	Decrease by seven: 60, 53, 46, 39, 32, 25, 18, 11. Increase by four: 3, 7, 11
	b	600 m	10mm = 2km, 3mm = 0.6 km = 600m
8	a	64 cm	One side = 12 + 4 = 16cm. Multiply by 4 for perimeter
	b	96 cm²	One triangle = 4 x 12 ÷ 2 = 24 cm², multiply by 4 for four triangles
	c	6	Area of large square = 16 x 16 = 256 cm². Area of small square = 256 − 96 = 160 cm². 160 ÷ 24 = 6.67, so only 6 triangles can fit into the square
9	a	30 min	Time = Distance ÷ Speed = 22km ÷ 44 kmh = 0.5 hours
	b	150 km/h	Distance between BC = 52 − 22 = 30km. Speed = 30 ÷ (12/60) hours = 150

Paper 3

	c	150 min	Speed from A to B was 44 km/h from part (a), CD = 22 km/h Distance from AD = 107 - 52 = 55 km Time = 55 ÷ 22 = 2.5 hours = 150 minutes
	d	33.44 km/h	Total Time = 0.5 + 0.2 + 2.5 = 3.2 hours, Distance = 107 km Speed = 107 ÷ 3.2 = 33.4375
10	a	80 points	Cycling = 130 min = 30pt, Running = 120 mins = 40pt, swimming = 14 mins = 10pt
	b	100 points	Cycling = 60 min = 35pt, Running = 140 mins = 35pt, swimming = 11 mins (<12 mins) = 30pt
	c	Swimming	Cycling = 180 min = 30pt, Running = 172 mins = 30pt Therefore Swimming = 100 - 60 = 40 points
	d	10 points	40 points each for Swimming and Running leaves 10 points for cycling to keep average at 30 points.
	e	70 points	Running = 30points which is 3X swimming 10 points Cycling = running = 30 points, therefore total of 70 points

Paper 4

1	a	135.35	143.22 - 7.87 = 135.35
	b	0.061	Largest to smallest: 1.0710, 1.0179, 1.0107, 1.0100 Tip - adjust all numbers to 4 dp to make it easier to sort
	c	6	$\frac{3}{24} + \frac{1}{24} = \frac{4}{24} = \frac{1}{6}$
2	a	£33	£231 ÷ 21 = £11 per ticket, so 3 tickets = £33
	b	5 hours 24 mins	0.675 x 40 = 27 students 12 mins x 27 = 324 mins ÷ 60 = 5.4 hours = 5 hours 24 mins
3	a	189	N = preceding number x3
	b	98	N = preceding number ÷ 2 + 1, so 50 -1 x 2 = 98
	c	8	N = preceding number ÷ 4 + 5, so 12 ÷ 4 + 5 = 8
4	a	5	20 sweets are shared in the ratio of 3:1 between mum and dad Therefore 15:5
	b	5	The sister ate a fifth of "what was left", i.e. 1/5 of a half = $\frac{1}{10}$ The parents ate remainder = $\frac{4}{10}$ = 20 sweets, so $\frac{1}{10}$ = 5 sweets
	c	50	$\frac{1}{10}$ = 5 sweets. So, 50 sweets
5	a	(8, 2)	The coordinates for '3' will be a reflection of the coordinates of '9' about the centre point (-4,2)
	b	(2, -4)	The distance between the centre point and circumference will be 6 i.e., radius = 6, so Y coordinate = 2 - 6 = -4
	c	37.68	2 x 3.14 x 6 = 37.68
	d	9.42	The distance between 12 and 3 is a quarter of the circumference, therefore 37.68 ÷ 4 = 9.42

Paper 4

6	e	18	Current radius = 6, so new radius 1.5 x 6 = 9 Diameter = 2 x radius = 18
	a	£72.75	Total Raised = 25.6 + 26.6 + 21 + 23.8 = £97 Ratio of 3:1, so Alpha receives three quarters
	b	Anne	Divide each amount raised by number of miles walked Oliver = 3.2, Anne = 3.8, Brett = 3.5, Yang = 3.4
	c	£24.25	Beta originally received $\frac{1}{4}$ of the proceeds. This will increase to a half of the total proceeds = 97 x ½ = 48.5 The question asks how much more, so, £24.25 more
	d	£17	Yang raised 3.4 per mile. Fran will raise 5 x 3.4 = £17
7	a	260 cm	5.98 = 2.3 x W, therefore W = 2.6m = 260 cm Check units of answer – do not accept 2.6m
	b	48.51 m²	Length = 1 + 5.1 + 6.4 - 2.6 from (a) = 9.9m Width = 3.8 + 1.1 = 4.9, therefore area = 9.9 x 4.9 = 48.51
	c	30.4 cm	(Length + Width) x 2 = (3.8 + (6.4-2.6)) x 2 = 15.2 m = 1520cm Scale is 1:50, so divide by 50 to get 30.4 cm
	d	86 planks	Area of lounge = (5.1 + 1) x 3.8 - kitchen area of 5.98 = 17.2 m² Area of plank = 1 x 0.2 = 0.2 m², planks needed = 17.2 ÷ 0.2
	e	£233.82	86 ÷ 5 = 17.2, therefore 18 whole packs required 12.99 x 18 = £233.82
8	a	$T = 280 + \frac{M}{50}$	280 is the fixed cost per year, and the variable cost per mile is $= \frac{£0.1}{5\ miles} = \frac{1}{50}$. **Note 280 + M x 0.02 is also acceptable**.
	b	£340	T = 280 + (3000 ÷ 50) = £340
	c	30,000 miles	(880 - 280) x 50 = 30,000
	d	23,500 miles	750 = 280 + (X ÷ 50), X = 23,500
	e	$T = 280 + \frac{M}{50} + 19d$	Additional charge = £19 per day, i.e., 19d Note M/50 = **0.02M** which is also acceptable

Paper 5

1	a	$\frac{5}{18}$	The common factor of 9 and 18 is 18, so $\frac{8}{9} = \frac{16}{18} - \frac{11}{18}$
	b	$4\frac{29}{40}$	$\frac{9}{4} \times \frac{21}{10} = \frac{189}{40}$, divide 189 by 40 = 4 r 29
	c	$\frac{12}{13}$	$\frac{16}{3} \times \frac{9}{52} = \frac{144}{156}$ = the common factor is 12
2	a	13.89	125 ÷ 9 = 13.89
	b	20.25 cm	Month 1 = 16 x 1.125 = 18, Month 2 = 18 x 1.125 = 20.25

Paper 5

	c	2 mins	Jill would have finished 3 minutes before Jack if they started at the same time. However, Jill started 5 mins later = 5 - 3
3	a	6 zeros	$\frac{1}{3}$ of 0.9 = 0.3 km² = 3,000,000m²
	b	5 m/s	18km per hour = 18,000 divide by 60 to convert into minutes and 60 again to calculate seconds
	a	12 mins	T = D/S = 14 / 70 = 0.2 hours = 12 mins
4	b	1.5 mins	80% of speed = 56mph. T = 7 / 56 = 0.125 hours = 7.5 mins. At 70mph, the second half would have taken 6 mins
	c	20 mph	Speed = D/T = 14 ÷ (42/60) = 14 ÷ 0.7 = 20 mph
	a	10 ml	18 months falls un the 1 to 2 years group. Max dose = 2.5ml 4 times a day = 10ml
5	b	6	10 y/o will have 10ml per dose. 3 doses = 10ml x 3 = 30ml. 30ml ÷ 5ml per spoon = 6 spoons
	c	9pm	Instructions state a minimum of 4 hours between doses. Timing of doses = 9am, 1pm, 5pm and 9pm
	a	▲ 4	Ratio of black to white = 3:2, so 20 shapes = 12:8 i.e.12 black. Ratio of triangle to square = 1:2, so 12 black shapes = 4:8
	b	■ 8	i.e., 4 black triangles and 8 black squares
6	c	△ 6	Ratio of black squares to white = 4:1. From (b) there are 8 black squares, so white squares = 2
	d	□ 2	As there were 20 shapes in the bag in total, 20 - 8 - 2 =14. 20 - 14 = 6 triangles remaining
	a	Average	
7	b	800 words	X axis = 20 mins, the first intersection with the 'fast; line is 800 mins. If after 20mins fewer words were typed, then average
	c	12 mins 30 secs	Y axis = 800 words, the first intersection with 'advanced' is in 12.5 minutes.
	d	Fast	553 + 653 = 603 words per 15 mins average. 615 falls under 'fast'. Anything lower than 600 falls under Ave.
	a	2n - 1	The number of triangles increase by 2 in each shape. The number of triangles is double 'N' and one less
8	b	21	N = (2 x 11) -1
	c	100	The number of black triangles is always = N
	d	585 cm²	The number of black triangles is always = N -1. Area = (40 - 1) x 15 cm² = 585 cm²
	a	25	64kg ÷ (1.6 x 1.6) m = 64 ÷ 2.56 = 25
9	b	80 cm	H² = 32kg ÷ 50 = 0.64. The square root of 64 is 8, therefore square root of 0.64 = 0.8
	c	86.7 kg	W = 30 x (1.7 x 1.7) = 86.7 kg
	d	4.5 kg	W = 30 x (1.5 x 1.5) = 67.5 kg. Her original weight is 72kg. 72 - 67.5 = 4.5kg

Paper 6

1	a	12 and -3	-3 x 12 = -36 and -3 + 12 = 9
	b	15 and 15	15-15 = 0 and 15+15=30
	c	$\frac{1}{2}$ and $\frac{1}{4}$	$\frac{1}{2} \times \frac{1}{4} = \frac{1}{8}$ and $\frac{1}{2} + \frac{1}{4} = \frac{3}{4}$
2	a	6	6.54 - 2.41 = 4.13, a difference of 3 from given answer 6 is the only digit that can be reduced by 3, to become 3
	b	8	27 + 51 +16 + 8 = 103, a difference of 5 from given answer 8 is the only digit that can be reduced by 5 to become 3
	c	4	416 + 75 = 491, a difference of 100 from given answer 4 in 426 is the only digit than can be reduced by 100 to 3
3	a	- 6	-5 x 2 = (-10) + (-2) = (-12) ÷ 2 = -6.
	b	15	18 x 2 = 36 ÷ 6 x 5 = 30 ÷ 2 = 15
4	a	£46.44	Total = £51.60, less 10% discount of £5.16 = £46.44
	b	£120	102 ÷ (85/100) = £120
	c	£6.95	Together: £69.5 x 2 = £139 x 0.85 = £118.15 with 15% off Separately: £139 x 0.90 = £125.10 with 10% off £125.10 – 118.15 = £6.95
5	a	55°	(A°+10°) + 90° + 25° = 180°
	b	145°	180° - (10° + 25°) =140°
	c	55°	C = A (on Z line) or 180° - 35° - 90° = 55°
6	a	0.155	(C - B) x D = (1.35 - 1.25) x 1.55 = 0.155
	b	False	The average of D and F is halfway i.e. E
7	a	8pm or 20:00	NY mall opens at 7am. Tokyo is 25 hours ahead, so local time in Tokyo is 8pm
	b	3 hours	Time difference between London and Tokyo is 8 hours. 8pm in London = 4am Tokyo. Mall opens in 3 hours at 7am.
	c	23:44 or 11:44pm	9:06pm + 7 hr 23min = 04:29 + 15 mins = 04:44 London time As NY is 5 hours behind London, the time in NY will be 23:44
	d	44 hours and 53 Mins	To arrive at 9am, the flight will have taken off 7hr 23 min earlier - therefore 1:37am London time, which is 8:37pm Thurs NY. From answer (c), calculate difference from Tues 11:44pm to Thurs 8:37pm = 16 min (Tues) + 24 hr (Weds) + 20:37 (Thurs)
8	a	30dw OR 30wd	30 x d x w = 30dw
	b	120 + 4wd + 4d	4 x (30 + w + d)
	c	25 cm	Volume = 30dw, 3750 = 30 x 5 x w w = 25

Paper 6

	d	2,050 cm²	2(30 x 25) + 2(30 x 5) + 2(25 x 5) = 2,050
	e	0.13 m²	2,050 - (30 x 25) = 1300 cm²
9	a	149.95 Euros	£130 x 1.13 = 146.9 (146.9 + 153) ÷ 2 = 149.95 Euros
	b	£40	339 ÷ 1.13 = £300 £300 - 130 - 130 = £40
10	a	33	X = 6n + 4, so 5th term of X = 34 Y = 85 − 3n, so 6th term of Y = 67 67 - 34 = 33
	b	9th term	X sequence = 10, 16, 22, 28, 34, 40, 46, 52, <u>58</u> Y sequence = 82, 79, 76, 73, 70, 67, 64, 61, <u>58</u> OR 6n+4 = 85 − 3n, so 9n = 81
	c	389	X: (100 x 6) + 4 = 604 Y: 85 - (3x100) = -215 604 − 215 = 389

Paper 7

1	a	83	17 - 11 x (- 6) = 17 - - 66 = 83
	b	6	6² ÷ 2(1 + 2) = 6² ÷ 2(3) = 36 ÷ 2(3) = 6
2	a	2	96 ÷ 8 = 12
	b	8 ÷ 2	8 ÷ 2 = 4
	c	1 + 6	28 ÷ 4 = 7 Digits not used in the calculation that add up to 7 are 1 & 6
3	a	120 km per hour	Multiply by 60 to convert minutes to hours: 2 x 60 = 120km
	b	33.3 or $33\frac{1}{3}$ m per sec	Cheetah travels 2000m (2km) per min Divide by 60 to calculate metres per second 2000 ÷ 60 = 33.33
	c	55 km	Cheetah: 2.5 hours x 120 = 300km Antelope: 2.5 x 98 = 245 km
4	a	143.08 cm	134.5 x 4% = 139.88cm + 3.2cm = 143.08
	b	1.4 m	Rebecca is 105% of the height her brother (1.47 ÷ 105) x 100 = 1.4
5	a	13 years	
	b	10 cm	170 cm - 160 cm
	c	15 years	If Peter is 4cm below his average height, then he should be 172cm tall. On the chart, 172 falls between 15 and 16
	d	18 years	Andy has a height of a 14y/o girl = 159 cm Add 15 cm = 174cm = height of 16 y/o boy Add 2 years = 18 years old

Paper 7

6	a	53	371 ÷ £7 = 53 children
	b	10 children	£7 x 70 children = £490. £540 - £490 = £50 was spent on lunch at £5 per child
	c	£119	£490 (70 children) - £371 (minimum cost) = £119
7	a	$61\frac{1}{3}$ cm	Month 2 = 23 x 2 = 46cm Month 3 = 46 x $1\frac{1}{3}$ = $61\frac{1}{3}$ cm
	b	$76\frac{2}{3}$ cm	Month 4 = $61\frac{1}{3}$ cm x $1\frac{1}{4}$ = $76\frac{2}{3}$
	c	$\frac{1}{5}$	Year 4 growth = 92cm - $76\frac{2}{3}$ = $15\frac{1}{3}$ $15\frac{1}{3}$ ÷ $76\frac{2}{3}$ = $\frac{1}{5}$
8	a	£41.42	3 standard hours + 2 hours overtime £25 + (2 x 8.21) = £41.42
	b	£49.26	Total number of overtime hours: Mon (2) Tues (1) Thurs (1) Fri (2) = 6 hours x £8.21 = £49.26
	c	26 hours	£25 x 5 days = £125 £210 - £125 = £85 £85 ÷ £8.21 = 10.35 - therefore 11 hours overtime needed 11 hours + 15 standard hours = 26 hours
9	a	n = 6 + 4(n - 1) or n = 4n +2	The first term starts at 6 and then each term increases by 4
	b	n = n²	The numbers shown are square numbers
	c	n = 5n - 3	
10	a	£19.98	£7.99 (pet photo) x 1.25 (frame) = £9.9875 x 2 photos = 19.975
	b	£24.19	Unframed photo = £12.50 Framed photo with parents = 12.50 x 1.15 (frame) = 14.375 10% Discount = 0.9 x (12.5 + 14.375) = 24.1875
	c	£33.89	3 x £8.50 + £12.50 x 1.15 = £39.875 <u>15% off total bill</u> (more than 3 photos) = 0.85 x 39.875 = 33.894
	d	£0.76	(3 x 6.25) + 12.5 x 1.15 = £33.125 = £33.13 Subtract from answer (c): 33.89 – 33.13 = 0.76

Paper 8

1	a	20	BODMAS: 4 - 8 ÷ 2 x (-4) 4 - 4 x -4 = 20
	b	-25	BODMAS: (-4) ÷ 2 x 7 -11 -2 x 7 - 11 = -25
	c	(8 ÷ 2) or (8 ÷ 2 x 7)	4 - (8 ÷ 2) x 7 - 11 = - 35

Paper 8

2	a	50	The children have 540 marbles in total, therefore should have 270 each. 320-270 = 50
	b	60	Peter has already given 50. By giving 10 more, Peter will have 260 and Jennifer will have 280 - a difference of 20
	c	108	Peter has 2/5 x 540 = 216 Jennifer has 3/5 x 540 = 324
3	a	17.92 m²	Kitchen length = twice width = 7.2 ÷ 2 = 3.6m Remove 0.8m from both L and W to calculate area of floor (7.2 - 0.8) x (3.6 x 0.8) = 17.92
	b	287 tiles	Area of 1 tile: 0.25 x 0.25 = 0.0625m² 17.92 ÷ 0.0625 = 286.72
	c	£1,112	Calculate # of packs needed = 287 ÷ 16 = 17.937 = 18 packs 18 packs x £34 = £612 + 500 = £1,112
	d	4 bottles	17.92 ÷ 5 = 3.584 litres of glue needed. Therefore 4 bottles required
	e	8 people	1 person = 8 days for half a kitchen 2 people = 8 days for full kitchen 4 people = 4 days, so 8 people to complete in 2 days
4	a	4 hours	Difference between 16:49 and 12:49
	b	Washington & Wellington	Thurs 7:49am and Fri 01:49am
	c	8:19 am Friday	12:49 + 11:30 mins = 00:19 Friday London time 00:19 + 8-hour time difference = 08:19
	d	03:22 am Saturday	08:19 + 5 hours = 13:19 take off 13:19 + 11hr 3 min = 00:22 Sat land Beijing time Add 3 hours to get Canberra local time
	e	11:22 am Friday	Washington is 16 hours behind Canberra 03:22 Sat - 16 hours = 11:22 Friday
5	a	36	$N = \frac{8}{2}(8 + 1) = 36$ balls
	b	$N = \frac{R^2}{2} + \frac{R}{2}$	Or $= \frac{R^2+R}{2}$
	c	31	The number of balls corresponds to the row number, e.g., row 2 has 2 balls, row 3 has 3 balls etc.
6	a	(6, 9)	Midway point between B:C = (14+4) ÷ c2 = 9 X point = 11 - 5 = 6
	b	(-4, -11)	C reflected in Y Axis = (-11, 4) Rotating 270° clockwise = 90° anticlockwise
7	a	2m	Height = Area ÷ Width = 0.9 ÷ 0.45 = 2m
	b	0.09m²	Height of Triangle = 2.4m – 2m = 0.4m Area = ½ x 0.45 x 0.4 = 0.09m²
	c	6 tubs	Area of 1 panel = 2 + 0.09 = 2.09 Area of both sides fence = 12 x 2.09 = 25.08 1 tub covers 5m², therefore six tubs are needed for the fence
	d	£285.74	Area of 15 fence panels = 2.09 x 15 = 31.35m Multiply by 2 for both sides = 31.35 x 2 = 62.7m Multiply by 2 again as painting 2 coats = 2 x 62.7=125.4m² 125 m² ÷ 5 = 25 tubs + 1 tub to cover 0.4m² = 26 tubs Cost = 26 x 10.99 = 285.74

Paper 8

8			
	a	32	Anne is 45 on the 26th May, so 44 on the 25th May 2034 2034-2022 = 12 years difference, so 44 - 12 = 32
	b	1989	2034 - 45 = 1989
	c	22 years 6 months	45 ÷ 2 = 22.5
	d	2030	Chis turns 22 ½ on 26 May 2034 Ben is 22 ½ - 8 years = 14 ½ on 26 May 2034 To get to age 11, reduce by 3 ½ year = Dec 2030
	e	51 years	We know on May 2034, Anne is 45, Chris 22 and Ben 14. May 2024 is 10 years earlier: Anne: 35, Chris 12, Ben 4 35 + 12 + 4 = 51

Paper 9

1	a	364.5	50% of 54 = 27 and = $\frac{1}{4}$ of 54 = 13.5 27 x 13.5 = 364.5
	b	31.2	BODMAS: 21.5 - 6.9 ÷ 3 + (12) 21.5 - 2.3 + 12 = 31.2
	c	$\frac{11}{26}$	5.5 is halfway between the numerators 5 and 6 Double both numerator and denominator
2	-	16	$3\frac{3}{7} \div \frac{3}{14} = \frac{24}{7} \div \frac{3}{14} = 16$
3	-	48	A + S = 67, where A = Adam and S = Son A + (A-29) = 67 2A = 96, so A = 48
4	a	829,892	The largest possible value of X = 749 The largest possible value of Y = 554 2XY = 2 x 749 x 554 =
	b	$\frac{545}{749}$	To get the smallest possible value of $\div \frac{X}{Y}$, Y has to be small as possible and X as large as possible Smallest possible value of Y = 545
5	a	£12.60	Book fine = 5 days x 30p = £1.50 x 2 books = £3 C fine = 8 days x 40p = £3.20 x 3 CD's = £9.60
	b	£4.10	Book 1 is due back on the 18th (5 days from 14th), 2 days late Book 2 is 16 days late (31 days in July) = 16 x 30p = £4.80 However, price capped at £3.50, so £3.50 + 2 x 30p = £4.10
	c	Mon 28th March	Total fine per day = 3 books x 30p + 1 CD x 40p = £1.30 £3.90 fine ÷ £1.30 = 3 days late so should have been returned on the 1st April. 5 days before 1st April = Mon 28th March
6	a	7:8	14 Girls: 14 + 2 Boys = 14:16 = 7:8
	b	180	(84 ÷ 7) x 8 = 96 boys 96 boys + 84 girls = 180 pupils in total
	c	12 teachers	Total number of students = 84 + 96 = 180 There is 1 teacher for every 15 students 180 ÷ 15 = 12

Paper 9

7	a	£8	10 x (10p + 20p + 50p) = £8
	b	2p	10 x (X + 20 + 50) = £7.20 X = 7.20 – 200 – 500 = 20p There are 10 coins replaced, so each coin must be 2p
8	a	2	12.5 - 2.5 - 8 = 2
	b	3.5	12.5 - 2 - 7 = 3.5
	c	4.5	12.5 - 3.5 - 4.5 = 4.5
	d	0	12.5 - 4.5 - 8 = 0
9	a	31	N = 3N + 1 where N = nth term and number of grey squares N = (3 x 10) + 1 = 31
	b	23	70 = 3N + 1, N = 23
	c	151	N = (3 x 50) +1
10	a	£25.30	(40 A3 x 0.25) + (50 A4 x 0.21) + (10 A4 x 0.18) + (20 A5 x 0.15) = £10 + £10.50 + £1.80 + £3 = £25.30
	b	£7.20	There are 120 prints in total. Colour = 60p extra for every 10 i.e. 6p for every print = 0.06 x 120 = 7.2
	c	17p	Current cost of 250 flyers = 50 x 25p + 200x 15p = £42.50 Average cost = 42.50 ÷ 250 = 17p
	d	£21.50	From part (c) the cost of 250 A3 flyers = £42.50 Remove 20% tax (0.2 x 42.50) = £8.50 Remove cost of flyers = (250 x 5p) = £12.50 Profit = 42.50 - 8.50 - 12.50 =
11	a	24.5 g	W = ((2 x 7) x 7 x 0.5) ÷ 2 = 24.5
	b	60 cm	300g = (30 x R x 0.5) ÷ 3 R = (300 x 3) ÷ (30 x 0.5) = 60
	c	8 mm	T = (H x R x 0.5) ÷ 50 = 40 x 20 x 0.5 = 400 ÷ 50 = 8
	d	1.96 kg	W = (35 x 35 x 0.5) ÷ 10mm = 61.25g 61.25 + 800 + 1100 =

Paper 10

1	a	$3\frac{3}{5}$	$\frac{4}{3} \times \frac{27}{10} = \frac{108}{30} = \frac{18}{5}$
	b	$1\frac{4}{51}$	$\frac{11}{3} \div \frac{51}{15} = \frac{165}{153} = \frac{55}{51} = 1\frac{4}{51}$
	c	$6\frac{23}{60}$	$5\frac{65}{60} - \frac{42}{60} = 6\frac{23}{60}$
2	-	420m	To get from $\frac{1}{4}$ of the distance to $\frac{1}{3}$ distance is 35 metres $\frac{1}{3} - \frac{1}{4} = \frac{1}{12}$ of distance = 35m x 12 = 420m

Paper 10

3	-	24 cm	Total length of string T1 = (L+8) + L $\frac{1}{4}$ of L = 2cm, so L = 8cm T = (8 + 8) + 8 = 24cm
4	a	£39.60	0.3 hours = 18 mins, so total hire time = 138 mins 30 min is fixed, so 108 ÷ 15 mins = 7.2, so 8 x 15 min intervals Cost = (30min at £13.20) + (8 x £0.8) + (4 x £5 jacket) = £39.60
	b	1 Hour	£29.80 - (3 x £5) - £13.20 = £1.60 £1.60 ÷ £0.80 = 2 x 15 mins = 30 min
	c	£11	Six friends mean two boats are needed (max 5 per boat) Cost of 1 boat = £13.20 + (6 x £0.80) = £18 = £36 for 2 boats 6 x £5 life jackets = £30. Total cost = £66, so cost per person = £11
	d	£122.60	Boat 1 = £13.20 + (2 x £0.80) = £14.80 Boat 2 = £13.20 + (4 x £0.80) = £16.40 Boat 3 = £13.20 + 4 x £0.80) = £16.40 15 life jackets = £75, so total cost = £122.60
	e	2 hours 15 Mins	39 min + 45 min + 39 min return = 123 mins However, as boat can only be hired in blocks of 15 mins after an hour, the required time is 135 mins = 2 hours
5	a	132 cm²	Internal square = 8 x 8 = 64 cm² External square = ((16 x 1) + (1 x 1)) x 4 = 68 cm²
	b	24 cm²	Th trapezium is made up of a square 4cm long and triangle 4 cm long. Area = (4 x 4) + (4 x 4 ÷ 2) = 24 cm²
	c	72 cm	4 x (8 + 8 + 1 + 1) = 72cm
6	a	32.3 pints	1 litre = 1.7 pints, so 3.8 litres = 3.8 x 1.7 = 6.46 pints 1 Gallon = 3.8 litres = 6.46 pints 5 gallons = 5 x 6.46 = 32.3 pins
	b	6.4 litres	Convert 8.5 pints to litres = 8.5/1.7 = 5 litres Convert 5 gallons to litre = 3.8 x 3 = 11.4 litres Difference = 11.4 - 5 = 6.4
7	a	£60.72	There is an 8% saving per pack when buying 10 or more £6 x (92/100) = £5.52 per pack £5.52 x 11 =
	b	9 %	(£6 - £5.46)= £0.54 ÷ £6 = 0.09
	c	£66.24	1 pack = 4 batteries and a pack can't be split as stated. 45 ÷ 4 = 11.25 packs, therefore 12 packs are needed 12 x £5.52 = £66.24
8	a	2.60, 2.57, 2.32, 2.29, 2.25	Each number rounded becomes: 2.32, 2.25, 2.60, 2.29 & 2.57 In descending order: 2.60, 2.57, 2.32, 2.29, 2.25
	b	15.450	Any number smaller that 15.450 (i.e., 15.449) would round down to 15.4
9	a	2hr 27 min	21 + 37 + 31 + 19 = 108min ÷ 4 = 27 min Average time all therefore 2 hours and 27 min
	b	2hr 20 min	Fastest two times = 2hr 19 and 2hr 21 Average = 2hr 20min
	c	1st	Total Time = (24 + 22 + 31 + 27) = 9hr 44min ÷ 4 = 2hr 26 min New Ave = 2hr 22min (4 min less) 2hr 22min x 5 = 9hr 44min + 5th runners time 5th runners time = 126 mins = 2hr 6min which is the fastest

Paper 10

10			
	a	2	Prime: 2, 3, 5, 7, 11, 13, 17, 19, 23 Square: 1, 4, 9, 16, 25 25 - 23 = 2
	b	72	Cube numbers: 1, 8 and third largest square number is 9 8 x 9 = 72
	c	4	5 + 11 = 16, 2 + 23 = 25, 2 + 7 = 9 and 3 + 13 = 16

11			
	a	3 cars	3 cars passed by in the 2nd minute
	b	7 cars	7 cars passed by in the 4th minute
	c	27 cars	6 + 3 + 5 + 7 + 6 = 26
	d	5 mins	

Paper 11

1			
	a	725	1450 is the smallest number that can be rounded to 1500 If we round 1449 to the nearest 100, the answer is 1400 As the original number was doubled, we need to halve 1450
	b	A = 8	A + B = 24 and 2= 2A. Substitute B with 2A A + 2A = 24, so A = 8
	c	300	D - C = 20, so D = 20 + C D + C = 40, so (20 + C) + C = 40, so C = 10 and D = 30

2			
	a	7	Substitute E + F with G and rearrange $\frac{E}{G}$ = 3 to E = 3G (E + F) x (G - E) becomes: G + (G - 3G) = -7, so G = 7
	b	-14	F = G - E and E = 3G, so F = G - 3G = -2G G = 7, so F = -2 x 7 = -14

3			
	a	84 °	1 hr = 360°, so 1 min = 6° 7 = 35 mins, so difference between 35 and 21 = 14 mins 14 x 6° = 84°
	b	9:41	840 ÷ 6° = 140 mins = 2 hours and 20 mins 7:21 + 2hs 20 = 9:41
	c	120 °	1 hr = 30°, so 4 hrs = 120°
	d	4	The number 7 is 35 mins past the hour 10:35, 11:35, 12:35, 1:35

| 4 | - | £330 | Ted spends $\frac{2}{3}$ on phone, so $\frac{1}{3}$ left over
He spends half of $\frac{1}{3}$ on shoes = $\frac{1}{6}$ of his saving = £55
So Saving = 55 x 6 = £330 |

Paper 11

5	a	$\dfrac{2}{3}$	Harry ate $\dfrac{1}{2}$ = 3 slices, George = $\dfrac{1}{3}$ = 2 slices Mike = 2 x Harry = 6 slices = 1 whole pizza 1 pizza – 1/3 = 2/3
	b	15 Slices	Fred = 2 slice less than Harry = 4 slices Slices eaten = 3 + 2 + 6 + 4 = 15 slices
	c	George	George ate 2 slices
6	a	A = 81°	As the shape is a parallelogram, the opposite angles are equal A + 5° = 86°, So A = 81°
	b	B = 33°	A + Y + X = 180° and Y = 2X, so substitute Y with 2X 180° = 81 + 3X, so X = 33°. B = X
	c	C = 49°	We know B = 33 and Z = 2C, so substitute into equation 180° = 33 + 2C + C, so C = 49°
7	a	False	A quarter of the girls ate apples
	b	False	Boys ate 75 apples and girls ate 150 oranges
	c	False	50 girls ate apples ($\dfrac{1}{4}$ of 200) compared to 75 boys
	d	True	25 boys ate oranges and 150 girls = 175
8	a	€12.78	$1 = €0.8, so $7.99 x 2 x 0.8 = 12.784
	b	176 CHF	$1.25 = €1 = 1 CHF, so $1 = 0.8CHF 220 * 0.8 = 176 CHF
	c	$100.68	23 CHF x 1.25 = $28.75 (1Euro = 1 CHF, 1CHF = 1.25 USD) €42 x 1.25 = $52.50 Total left over = 23 + 52.5 + 19.43 = $100.68
9	a	6.25 cm	100 ÷ 16 = 6.25cm
	b	20 pieces	50 ÷ 2.5 = 20
	c	15 cm	50cm remaining – ratio 2:3:5 = 10:15:25 Difference = 25 – 10 = 15
10	a	3 cm	The centres are 7cm apart but with 1cm gap. So, the radius = 3cm, therefore diameter = 6cm
	b	45°	The triangle is right angled, so the 2 angles will be equal 180 – 90 = 90°, so X = 45°
	c	13 cm	1cm + (2 x Diameter) = 1+ 2 x 6 = 13cm
	d	37.47 cm	Circumference = 2 x 3.24 x 3cm = 18.84cm per circle 1 ¾ circles x 18.84 = 32.97cm + 4.5 =

Paper 12

1	a	24, 31, 38, 45	52 − 17 = 35 To calculate the increments, 35 ÷ 5 = 7
	b	3, 15	Each number is the multiple of the previous two numbers Second digit: 900 ÷ 60 = 15 i.e., 15 x 60 = 900 First digit: 15 ÷ 5 = 3
2	a	10 eggs	Note, question asks 'On the 5th day' – not 'by' the 5th date Black: 3 eggs on 5th day White: 5 eggs on 5th day Brown and Brown don't lay eggs on the 5th day
	b	24 eggs	The black hen lays 3 eggs daily, so 3 will hatch on days 21 to 28 = 8-day x 3 = 24
	c	Red Hen	Calculate how many eggs would normally be collected on day 7 Black: 3 eggs + White: 5 eggs = 8 eggs Red will lay on days 1, 3, 5, 7, so 2 eggs Brown will lay on days 1, 4, 7, so 4 eggs 3 + 5 + 2 + 4 = 14 eggs normally on day 7. As Giles collects 12 eggs, he's sold the hen which lays 2 eggs
3	a	30%	105 ÷ 350 = 0.3 = 30%
	b	15%	(£119.60 - £104) = £15.6 profit on each bike ÷ £104 cost price = 0.15 x 100 = 15% profit
	c	Pazazz	Pazazz = 63 bikes x £193.50 = £12,190.50 Townsend = 98 bikes x £ 119.60 = £11,72.80
	d	Chicco an Pedal pals	40% of 350 bikes sold = 140 Chicco (35 bikes) and Pedal Pals (105 bikes)
4	a	(11, 5)	As this is an isosceles triangle, distance from AB = BC X-axis AB = 7 − 3 = 4. So BC = 7 + 4 = 11 Y-axis of point C = y-axis point A = 5
	b	(-3, 5)	A = (3, 5), reflected in Y-Axis =
	c	(-12, 7)	270° clockwise = 90° anti clockwise, B= (7, 12)
	d	(5, 8.5)	Centre point on X axis between 3 and 7 is 5 Centre point on Y axis between 5 and 12 is 8.5
5	a	21 cm	The area of one square is 9cm², so one side is 3cm long Width = 3 + 6 + 3 + 6 + 3 = 21 cm
	b	270 cm³	Volume of one brick = 9 x 6 = 54 cm³ Volume of model = 54 x 5 = 270
	c	378 cm²	Surface area of 1 block = (9 x 2) + 4 x (6 x 3) = 90cm² x 5 = 450 Subtract sides not visible i.e., where the blocks connect 9cm² x 8 square cut outs = 72cm²
	d	31 blocks	Every 2 blocks are 9cm long (3cm + 6cm) 138 – first block = 135cm. 135 ÷ 9 = 15 lots of 2 blocks = 30 blocks + first block
6	a	1.125 l	For every 4 parts, 3 will be water, i.e. $\frac{3}{4}$ ¾ x 1500 ml = 1,125 ml
	b	250 ml	For every 6 parts, 1 will be screen wash, i.e. $\frac{1}{6}$ 1/6 x 1500 ml = 250ml
	c	$833\frac{1}{3}$ ml	$\frac{2}{3}$ of 1.5l = 1l x $\frac{5}{6}$ = 833.33 ml
	d	Summer	Because for each 1.5 litre, you would use $\frac{1}{6}$ instead of ¼ screen wash

Paper 12

7	a	142,330 mm	M to cm = x100, cm to mm = x 10 142.33 x 1000 = 142,330
	b	140 g	Two packs of teabags weight ¾ of 80g = 60g Total weight = 80 + 60 = 1.4kg
	c	2 kg	W = weight of crate and O = full crate of oranges W + O = 23 and W + $\frac{O}{3}$ = 9 O = 23 - W, so W + $\frac{23-W}{3}$ = 9 3W + 23 − W = 27, so 2W = 4
8	a	54 mins	Time = Distance ÷ Speed Uphill = 9 miles ÷ 15 = 0.6 hours x 60 = 36 mins Downhill is half the time = 18 min
	b	20 mph	Total time = 36+18 = 54 mins = 0.9 hours Total Distance = 9 + 9 = 18 miles Ave Speed = 18 ÷ 0.9 = 20 miles per hour
9	a	125	5 x 5 x 5 = 125
	b	Either answer of 34 or 81	Find any multiple of 81, e.g. 3 or 9 then calculate how many times it has to be multiplied by itself to get to 81 34 = 3 x 3 x 3 x 3 or 92 = 9 x 9 = 81
	c	Either answer of 82 or 26	43: 4 x 4 x 4 = 64 82: 8 x 8 = 64 26: 2 x 2 x 2 x 2 x 2 x 2 = 64
	d	25	To get to 9 we can either use 32 (3x3) or 91 (9x1) 2 is a multiple of 32, and 2x2x2x2x2 = 32, so 25 is starting number

If you require a more detailed response to a question or how an answer has been derived, please email info@bgsbooks.com and one of our experts will be happy to provide a response.

Printed in Great Britain
by Amazon